7-12-77
7.90

Grains

GRAINS

An Illustrated History with Recipes

Elizabeth Burton Brown

Prentice-Hall, Inc.

ENGLEWOOD CLIFFS ❧ NEW JERSEY

Frontis: *F. A. O. Photo by F. Botts*

F. A. O. photo by F. Botts

Printed in the United States of America   •J

Prentice-Hall International, Inc., London
Prentice-Hall of Australia, Pty. Ltd., North Sydney
Prentice-Hall of Canada, Ltd., Toronto
Prentice-Hall of India Private Ltd., New Delhi
Prentice-Hall of Japan, Inc., Tokyo
Prentice-Hall of Southeast Asia Pte. Ltd., Singapore

10 9 8 7 6 5 4 3 2 1

Library of Congress Cataloging in Publication Data

Brown, Elizabeth Burton, 1916–
  Grains.

  Bibliography: p.
  Includes index.
  SUMMARY: A history of fifteen ancient and modern
cultures focusing on their food and a discussion of
edible grains, their preparation, and consumption
throughout history. Recipes included.
  1. Cereals as food — History — Juvenile literature.
2. Cookery (Cereals) — Juvenile literature. [1. Cereals
as food — History. 2. Cookery — Cereals] I. Title.
TX393.B86   641.3'31'09   76-10223
ISBN 0-13-362269-X

To my husband, Delbert,
who faithfully tested the product of each recipe.

Contents

Grains

❧ 1 ❧
"Lo, Here Is Seed for You"

Twelve thousand years ago, when the ice and snow covering the earth began to melt, new rivers flowed into fertile valleys with budding apple trees, wild berries, root vegetables, peas and beans. Once again warm breezes blew grain into golden waves across the land. Seeds from the grain were to become the major source of food for mankind.

However, primitive man ignored the grasses when he first walked upon the earth. He ate only tiny animals. The ancestors of wheat, barley, oats, corn, rye, and rice had been growing millions of years before man's arrival. Dinosaurs (who preceded him) also ignored grasses; instead they tore huge ferns and trees out of the ground for their nourishment. Only small animals, which primitive man killed for food, ate grains and grasses. The tiny horse, here before the grasses, started to eat the grains when they appeared. His teeth began to grow large to obtain nourishment from the branches of shrubs and became flat to grind the grain that he preferred. In time, his new diet made him grow larger and become a fast runner.

Then the world grew colder and the last ice age began. Dinosaurs and the ferns and trees they feasted upon died; only small animals that could stand the cold endured. The grasses and other plants bearing seeds flourished and evolved into stronger types. Their seeds had an outer coat to protect them

1

from cold and water. They remained dormant under the ice, always ready to sprout into a new plant when the earth was warmed by the sun. They traveled great distances on the wing of a bird, the back of an animal, or in the wind. As the years passed, airborne seeds must have lodged in areas that were untouched by the glaciers that covered half of the world. Wild grasses grew easily in warm or cold places, and they did not require a great deal of water. They were able to reseed themselves, because their seeds scattered when the plant ripened.

Grazing animals went where the grains grew. The type of grain they found depended upon the geography and climate of the land. Rice grew in very damp places all across the southern part of Asia, wheat grew wild in the Near East, oats and rye in the colder north of Europe, barley in central Europe, millet and sorghum in Africa, and corn in Central America. Wherever the animals went, man followed, but he did not eat raw grain because he could not digest it as well as raw meat.

When he finally learned to use fire for cooking as well as for warmth, he sprinkled roasted grain seeds on the meat that he roasted or steamed in pit fires to give it a pleasant nutty flavor. He roasted the grain seeds on a hot rock, discovering that the indigestible chaff or outer hull parted more easily from the kernel because cooking the grains made them brittle. Adding a little water to the cooked grain and keeping it warm until the seeds sprouted made a kind of porridge that could be easily digested.

No one knows how our prehistoric ancestors discovered the nutritional value of grain. It must have taken years of trial and error to determine which grasses could be eaten profitably. The seeds of cereal—wheat, barley, oats, rye, rice, millet, sorghum, corn—contain the protein, carbohydrates, minerals, and vitamins essential for life.

Women and children who gathered seeds probably noticed that larger plants grew where refuse was piled outside the camps and caves and where the soil was loose and soft. As a

Bread making in the days of primitive man.
American Magazine, May, 1879. Published by Frank Leslie. New York Public Library, Picture Collection.

result, they planted a few seeds on the well-fertilized soil to have a better supply of food.

Agriculture began when men realized it would be better to control the harvest of grains by planting seeds at a definite season, rather than gathering by chance. They learned to select seeds from the best plants and to sow them in an orderly manner and in prepared soil. At first, a pointed stick was used to loosen the earth. Stone hatchets or weights of stone were added to make the digging easier. When the plants were ripe, it was not difficult to cut the grain stalks with a sickle made of stone and then beat the tops to shake out the grain.

Rubbing the roasted grain seeds between two stones made a coarse flour. The addition of water made a paste that was easier to swallow. Some of the paste must have dropped on a flat rock to bake. The result was a flatbread similar to a pancake, the oldest type of bread. In some parts of the world, bread is still made in the same manner. *Chapatis* are made in India of wheat flour and water. *Tortillas* are made in many areas of Mexico as they were centuries ago of flour made of parched corn. In Scotland, flatbreads made of oats and water are called *bannocks.* Flatbreads called *injera* are baked in Africa from the ground seeds of millet. In each case the grain is different, but the principle is the same.

Each grain has a fascinating story. In this book, I have presented the stories of cereals, the grains that are prepared for food by mankind. To be more fully acquainted with the foods and cooking of other peoples, we need to cook and eat the foods they make. The standard equipment of the American kitchens can be used in almost every recipe with a bit of improvisation. We shall note how civilization began with the cultivation of a few seeds and that:

> *While the earth remaineth, seedtime and harvest, and cold and heat, and summer and winter, and day and night shall not cease.* (Genesis 8:22)

Chapatis

The mother of a family in India generally grinds enough flour from her store of wheat to make a day's supply of *chapatis* for her own family. She grinds the grain between two stones and mixes the coarse flour with water in the evening. The next morning she kneads the dough, divides it into small portions about the size of a golf ball, and rolls them out on smooth wood with a rolling pin and cooks them over glowing coals on a griddle called a *tava.*

The *chapatis* are used instead of forks for placing food in the mouth. Properly, a small piece of the bread is broken off and wrapped around food in a bowl with the fingertips of one hand. The bland taste of the bread makes an interesting contrast to the spicy curry that is part of the Indian cuisine.

An old and secret way of sending messages around the country is sometimes used when runners take specially folded *chapatis* between villages. The way they are folded or divided may indicate a secret date or event that is to occur.

❧CHAPATIS

Ingredients	*Utensils*
Whole wheat flour	Griddle
All-purpose flour	Rolling pin
Water	Mixing bowl
Salt	Damp cloth
	Measuring cups or metric measuring containers

RECIPE

Standard	*Metric*
1/4 cup all-purpose flour	35 grams
1/4 cup whole wheat flour	30 grams
1/4 cup water	60 ml
Pinch of salt	

METHOD

Place flour and salt in a bowl. Gradually add the water and stir to form a firm dough. Knead the dough for five minutes. Roll it into a ball and cover with a damp cloth. Leave it alone for a half hour, as resting the dough relaxes the gluten and makes it easier to roll out.

Place the griddle on medium heat. Divide the dough into six pieces the size of a golf ball. Keep them covered with a damp cloth. Take one out at a time. Flatten and roll on surface that has been dusted with whole wheat flour. If the rolling pin is applied with equal pressure on all sides from the center out, a thin circle about five inches in size will be formed. Don't be disturbed if the first one or two are a little difficult to roll.

Cook them quickly on both sides on an ungreased griddle. Place under the broiler on aluminum foil for a minute to make them puff up.

Serve immediately with butter.

Yield: 6.

Bannocks from Scotland

A *bannock* in the Gaelic language of Scotland is an oatcake. Scots call a griddle a *girdle*; they were made of iron and suspended over the fire in the center of the old stone cottages. There was no chimney, just a small opening for the escaping smoke. Scots still serve *bannocks* with a bit of fish or cheese or marmalade. Oats grew wild in this beautiful land. Part of the equipment of a Scottish soldier was a small bag of oatmeal and a metal plate. He sometimes existed for days on oatcakes.

An old legend about King Alfred of England tells of the time that he watched the bannocks cook as a favor to an old woman in her cottage. At the time, Alfred was planning a way to save his country from the invading Danes. Since he was weary, he asked the lady of the cottage if he might rest a while. Not knowing who he was, she gave her consent, if he would agree to watch her bannocks cooking on the griddle while she went on a short errand. So concerned was he with his own thoughts that he forgot all about the roasting oatcakes. When she returned they were burned, and the old lady scolded him severely. He took the scolding very meekly and never told her who he was. A monument has been built in England in memory of his humility.

❧BANNOCKS

Ingredients	Utensils
Oatmeal	Blender
Water	Griddle
Salt	Metal spatula
Butter	Rolling pin
	Measuring cups or metric measuring containers

RECIPE

Standard	Metric
1 1/2 cups oatmeal finely ground	180 grams
1/4 cup hot water	60 ml
1 tablespoon butter	15 grams
Pinch of salt	

METHOD

Grind the oatmeal for a few minutes in the blender. Add water, butter, and salt and knead on a floured counter until the ingredients are well blended. Divide the dough into two portions. Roll each portion into a circle about six inches wide and 1/8 inch thick. Cut the circles into fourths and then cut each fourth in half. Place each triangular piece on a hot griddle. Bake until the edges slightly curl. Turn on the other side and bake for two minutes.

Remove and place on a tea towel to cool. Serve with butter and cheese.

Bannocks may be baked in a 350° F (177° C) oven for 20 minutes, but a griddle baking is more authentic.

Yield: 16.

Corn Tortillas of Mexico

Corn grew wild 7500 years ago in the Tehuacan Valley, south of Mexico City, Mexico. Each kernel was wrapped separately in its own husk. They were lightly attached to ears that were only one-half inch in length. The kernels could easily scatter on the ground to reproduce new plants.

The Indians who lived in caves above the valley gathered the corn and developed it into a type that is similar to modern corn with a larger ear of kernels wrapped in a single husk and dependent upon man for planting.

Eventually, the cultivation of corn by other Indian tribes spread throughout North and South America. They called it the gift of the gods and it was the basis of their diet.

The ancient Mexicans cooked the hard kernels in water with charcoal added to soften them. They ground them into a paste and added more water to make a dough for their flatbreads that were called *tortillas* by the Spanish. They slapped small pieces of the dough between their hands until they were in the shape of thin circles and baked them on a griddle called a *comalli.*

Tortillas are a welcome part of every meal in Mexico. In some areas, wheat flour is used rather than *masa* (cooked ground corn).

Note: Since ordinary masa must be used immediately to prevent souring, Instant Masa or Masa Harina (made by Quaker Oats Co., Chicago, Illinois) is preferable. A wheat flour recipe is included for use if Instant Masa is not available.

❧CORN TORTILLAS

Ingredients	*Utensils*
Masa Harina	Griddle
Water	Rolling pin
	Bowl
	Wax paper
	Measuring cups or metric measuring containers

RECIPE

Standard	*Metric*
1 cup masa	120 grams
1/2 cup water	120 ml

METHOD

Combine masa and water in a bowl. With your hands work the mixture well until the masa and water are well blended—about five minutes. Divide the dough into six pieces the size of a golf ball. Place a 12-inch-square sheet of wax paper on counter. Place one section of dough on it. Cover with another sheet of wax paper. Roll the dough out into a circle between the two sheets of wax paper. Repeat with other portions.

Bake on an ungreased hot griddle on each side until they are lightly browned.

Yield: 6.

❧WHEAT FLOUR TORTILLAS
(as made by Dolly Castro from her mother's recipe)

Ingredients	*Utensils*
All-purpose flour	Bowl
Baking powder	Griddle
Salt	Rolling pin
Shortening (vegetable)	Wooden spoon
Water	Measuring spoons
	Measuring cups or metric measuring containers

RECIPE

Standard	Metric
5 cups flour	700 grams
2 teaspoons baking powder	10 grams
2 teaspoons salt	10 grams
3 tablespoons shortening	45 grams
1 3/4 cups warm water (90°–100°)	420 ml

METHOD

Sift flour and baking powder and salt in a bowl. Add shortening. Blend it into the flour with your hands. Slowly add warm water and stir with a wooden spoon. Then blend the mixture thoroughly by working it together with your hands. Form into about 16 balls the size of a golf ball. Let each rest 20 minutes until the gluten in dough relaxes. Flatten into 3-inch circles with your hands and then roll each from the center out with a rolling pin on a floured counter. They should be thin and five or six inches in diameter.

Cook on ungreased griddle preheated on medium heat. Cook on each side until slightly brown blisters are formed.

Yield: 16.

❧BURRITOS

A Mexican sandwich of tortillas wrapped around a filling.

Ingredients	*Utensils*
Tortillas—either homemade or purchased at grocery store (1 package)	Knife for chopping
	Sauce pan
	Griddle
Chopped cooked meat or chicken or cooked ground round (1 lb or 500 grams)	Several bowls

Salsa Verde (Chili sauce)
Tomato sauce
Green chili—either fresh or canned
Garlic
Onion
Salt
Grated cheese
Shredded lettuce

RECIPE FOR SALSA VERDE
Tomato sauce (16 oz or 430 grams)
1 hot green chili, chopped
1 small garlic clove, chopped
1 small onion, chopped
Salt (1/2 teaspoon or 3 grams)

METHOD
Heat all the ingredients for Salsa Verde in a sauce pan. Simmer slowly for 10 minutes. Serve from bowl so that each may take according to taste and placement in the sandwich.

Place 1/2 pound grated cheese (yellow), 1 head of shredded lettuce, the chopped onion, and the cooked meat in separate bowls.

Reheat tortillas on ungreased skillet. Keep them warm in covered baking dish. Uncover for serving. Let each make his own burrito.

Serves 6.

2

"And Ye Shall Sow the Land"

Wild wheat grew abundantly on the hills north of the Tigris and Euphrates river valleys where rain made irrigation unnecessary and the weather was pleasant and mild, streams were plentiful, and the land had been protected from glacier and flood.

For thousands of years, caves in the area had served as the dwelling places for prehistoric families, but around 7000 B.C. some people decided to live near the wheat fields permanently and gather the seed for food. They built a village of small, square mud homes, they cut the ripe grain with stone sickles, and planted new crops from some of the seeds of the best plants. After the wheat was harvested, it was stored in reed baskets ready to be ground into flour between two stones. The larger stone had a round depression on its surface. The wheat placed in the slight well was rubbed back and forth by someone pushing a smaller stone over it.

The village and the people who lived there were unknown to the modern world until 1955. In 1948 Prof. Robert J. Braidwood, strolling on a mound in the area, noticed pieces of broken flint on the ground. He reasoned that the stones might be the remnants of old farming tools. Return trips with a group of other archeologists in 1950 and 1955 proved his theory to be correct. They unearthed the village, now named Jarmo. It is considered to be the home of the first farmers in the world, the place where man ceased to be a wanderer and became a food cultivator. Other settlements have been found in the general area. In addition to stone tools and some crude pottery, they found the remains of wheat as wild and untamed as the kind that still grows on the hillside and a type of domesticated wheat similar to that grown today. It was stronger and had less brittle heads because it was cultivated from selected seeds. The grains were given radiocarbon tests that dated them as old as 7000 years.

One of the side effects of the nuclear bomb program of the 1940s was the discovery of carbon 14, a new key to measure the age of bone or plant material uncovered by archeologists. It seems that all living things receive a radioactive carbon from the atmosphere. When death occurs, the process stops and the balance of carbon 14 (as it is known) is no longer the same as that in the atmosphere. A radioactive decay slowly begins that reduces carbon 14 to ordinary carbon. The change does not occur overnight. Before one half of the carbon 14 becomes ordinary carbon, 5,700 years pass; 11,500 years before three-fourths of the carbon is changed to ordinary carbon, and so on in the same proportion.

Because of this new type of measurement of the age of relics, we know that Europe was inhabited by a type of man at least 500,000 years ago, Asia about 250,000 years ago, and that another type, similar to modern man, replaced him about 35,000 years ago. He wore clothing that he fashioned with fine bone needles. About 9000 years ago he started to farm in the Near East, and perhaps a little later in India, China, and Central America. It has been noted that his appearance changed when he began to eat grains for food. The heavy jaws and huge teeth needed to devour partially cooked or raw meat gradually became smaller because they were not needed for the chewing of cereals.

When archeologists study an area, they do not work carelessly with picks and shovels. They enclose a portion of the ground within wooden frames and scratch the soil within the frames with small instruments, even teaspoons and brushes. Photographs are taken before any object is removed. Stones, bones, pieces of pottery are then carefully removed and numbered and classified for study. Dirt is carefully sifted. Plant spores and seeds are separated for microscopic viewing.

Jarmo was never more than a village in the hills. About two hundred people lived there in small houses. Each family sowed about two acres of wheat which furnished them enough for almost a year. Excess grain was stored underground in baskets that had been covered with clay. Sometimes the grain was boiled in bowls of stone. Burghul (or bulgur), as it is called, is still a favorite dish in the Near East. Sometimes ground lamb was added and pounded with the wheat grain and cooked with it.

Sheep were the first animals to be domesticated. They were probably forced into a rocky ravine. The approach was barricaded afterward. A few were allowed to live through the winter; they were fed and thus became tame. Wild goats, pigs, and cattle were also domesticated by the same process. Of course, we can only conjecture on the method, but we do know that the strong ox helped pull the plow and trample the grain in order to thresh it.

A host of other steps soon followed. Pottery replaced the crude baskets, clay ovens were made, but hot flat stones still sufficed as griddles for a kind of pancake made of flour, sesame seeds, and onions. Peasants in Iraq enjoy them today.

A similar sequence of events took place in the city of Jericho in Palestine. The people apparently devoted a great deal of their energies to building a wall to make their brick dwelling places permanent and safe from attack.

Some of the people who settled in or near Jarmo moved into the flat plain at the delta of the Tigris and Euphrates rivers. The area was generally called Mesopotamia, which means

14

Babylonian inscriptions. Tablets of baked clay with cuneiform inscriptions recording business transactions. *The Metropolitan Museum of Art, Gift of Matilda W. Bruce, 1907.*

"land between two rivers" in Greek. Silt from the rivers was deposited at the deltas to form especially fertile soil near the Persian Gulf. Palm trees bearing nutritious dates lined the rivers. Such a "garden of Eden" attracted many people. Because no rain fell during the year, an elaborate system of ditches and canals was built to carry water from the rivers to ever widening rows of fields that spread out into the desert.

Farming became so successful that there was an abundance of wheat and thus it could begin to be traded or bartered for other commodities. Because this required a method of recording the transactions, a form of writing was invented, which was later adopted by other ancient civilizations in the Near East. It was quite different from our writing. Paper was unknown, therefore impressions were made upon wet clay tablets with a square-tipped reed called a *stylus.* (Because the resulting marks were wedge-shaped, the script has been called *cuneiform* from a Latin word *cuneus,* meaning wedge.) The tablets were then baked in the sun or fired in an oven. They have endured through the centuries, and thousands have been uncovered in the dry sands of the region.

Many scholars spent long and patient hours trying to decipher them. Finally in 1847, the key to the cuneiform was found. An Englishman named Rawlinson copied some inscriptions he found high on the steep side of a rock, called Behistun, in Iran, or old Persia. The message was written in three languages: Persian, Elamite (a province of old Persia), and cuneiform of ancient Mesopotamia. By translating the Persian first, the ancient cuneiform meaning was revealed. The signs were learned and other inscriptions and tablets were successfully translated.

It was a very difficult system to write. Many signs had to be memorized. A few of the people were educated and trained to be scribes: they wrote the official documents.

Rather than farm, some of the people became scribes to write the laws, some built and designed bridges and canals to irrigate the fields, and some became teachers to instruct others in mathematics, astronomy, or agriculture.

One day a father wrote with a stylus upon wet clay to his son. He started his clay tablet by saying, "In days of yore a farmer gave these instuctions to his son." He then told him all that he felt he should know in order to harvest a good crop of wheat or barley: that the water should not be too high when the field was being irrigated, that the oxen should not trample the wet mud after the fields had been inundated, that he should clear the fields of weeds and plant a fence around them, and to have all his tools ready and in order. Furthermore, he warned him to watch the laborers so they did not shirk their jobs or plant the grain unevenly. He advised him to cut the grain before it became overly ripe and to thresh it by drawing a threshing sledge back and forth over the stalks for five days. Before the grain was bagged, it must be tossed in the air with pitchforks to free it from dirt. This instruction has been called "the first *Farmer's Almanac*."

Another "first" of Mesopotamia was "Gilgamesh," the first legend that was ever written. In it is related the story of a flood, similar to the one in the Bible. It tells us that one of the characters in the story ate peas and beans as well as dates, meat, and a kind of pancake. Gilgamesh was the legendary

Hittite, c. 1200 B.C. Provenance: Tell Halaf. Relief: carved face and end; face: Gilgamesh (?) Basalt.

The Metropolitan Museum of Art, Rogers Fund, 1943.

king of Urak, a city six miles in length, with streets wide enough for chariots, fine homes for the wealthy, smaller homes for the farmers who went outside of the city walls to work in their fields.

By 3000 B.C., there were several cities with surrounding farmlands close enough to the rivers to tap their precious gift of water by canals and smaller channels. Some controlled the area for a time. Sumer, Akkad, Babylon, and Assur were the kernels of later empires. Conflicts arose when a particular area seemed to have more wealth than another.

Each city-state was dedicated to a special god who had his own temple within the city walls. Often the temples were placed on artificial mountains or ziggurats. The Biblical Tower of Babel is an example. Granaries were built near the temples.

17

Mesopotamian (Assyrian) IX Century B.C. Winged being worshipping the sacred tree, and eagle-headed, winged beings pollinating the sacred tree. Alabaster. From the Palace of Ashur-nasir-apal II (885-860 B.C.) King of Assyria, at Kalhu.

The Metropolitan Museum of Art. Gift of John D. Rockefeller, 1932.

At first priests were in charge of the granaries and planting of the crops. The farmers had to contribute a portion of their crops to the city gods and the communal welfare. Barley was used as money. The use of an ox for three days threshing cost 3/4 quart of barley. In a short time, kings usurped the power of the priests.

Most historians believe that Mesopotamia was the first area of farming, and that its influence on the rest of the world is unquestionable. Because of a growth in population, agriculturalists moved to other areas, or other food gathering people received the idea from them. There were farmers in Greece in 6000 B.C., in Italy and in the area of the Danube River around 5000 B.C. Even as far north as the North Sea and Scotland where it is colder people were farming around 4000 B.C. The only difference was that a type of grain was cultivated that would grow in colder climates — oats or rye.

People moved eastward as well as across the Mediterranean Sea into Europe. Iran lies directly east of Iraq. It is like a huge saucer of arid land between Mesopotamia and the Indus River on the border of present-day India and Pakistan. Ancient farming villages were scattered across the Iranian plateau. Many centuries ago the people learned to irrigate the land by digging a series of wells on the sloping land near the mountains. The wells were connected by tunnels that sloped just enough to carry the water toward a destination that might be a hundred miles away from the first well. The tunnels, called *ghanats* or *kanats*, were dug many feet below the earth's surface. They are still used today to irrigate wheat, barley, rice, and other crops grown in Iran. They must be cleaned regularly to keep them free from sediment.

But it was on the Indus River that the most amazing civilization appeared. Here were carefully planned cities with huge granaries, streets with fine drainage, and homes with adequate kitchens and bathrooms. The people who lived there cultivated wheat about one thousand years later than those who

lived in Mesopotamia. They may have been the first to cultivate rice, which we will discuss in more detail in Chapter Five.
They were the first to cook vegetables and to season them with
a blend of spices ground in a mortar and pestle (curry). They
grew oranges, lemons, and bananas, raised goats, pigs, and
cattle. It was they who domesticated a little wild jungle fowl
into the chicken. Only recently have scientists known about
these people in greater detail. Several excavations were made
in the area in the 1920s.

We have a written record in the Bible of an individual who
migrated from Ur, a very sophisticated city in Mesopotamia, to
eventually become the father of a new nation of people who
believed in one God. They are the Israelites and their founder
Abraham. The Old Testament mentions Abraham's hospitality
as he traveled on the desert. Three visitors appeared at his
tent at the Oaks of Mamre where he and his family were camped.
As was the custom, he bade his wife Sarah to bake flat
cakes of fine meal for them on a hot rock. Meanwhile, he prepared a calf for them. It was necessary to eat meat immediately
after it was killed because of the desert heat. Today the
Bedouins of the desert prepare their food in the same manner.

The record further states that some of Abraham's descendants lived in Egypt for a while because of a shortage of grain
in their area. After many years and a great deal of misery they
returned to the land of Canaan to continue a life of farming.
Their Exodus from Egypt under Moses' guidance is well
known, as well as his ascent up the mountain to receive the
Ten Commandments, the basis of Judaic law. It seemed that
he was up there for a long time. So long that the people who
were waiting for him found that the cream that was a part of
their daily nourishment had turned sour. To this day, cheese
blintze served with sour cream is a traditional dish. Unleav-
ened bread is traditionally served on the Passover to com-
memorate the Exodus. The Israelites were forced to leave
Egypt in such a hurry that there was not time for the bread to

rise. Apparently they had discovered the secret of yeast from the Egyptians, whose progress we shall discuss in the next chapter.

When the Israelites returned to the land of Canaan, they transferred some of the farming techniques that they had learned in Egypt to the Promised Land. The flat and well-watered lands near the coast had no need of an irrigation system. It was a productive wheat belt. Wheat typifies the best food in Old Testament literature.

Seedtime in Israel was the period from early October until early December. Harvest was in April, when the American farmer now is spading and seeding his plot. The harvest season lasted fifty days, beginning with Passover in April and ending with the Feast of Ingathering or Pentecost in June. As on the banks of the Nile, seed was sown with little soil preparation and trodden by the feet of cattle into the soil. If the land was cultivated, the implements were primitive and inefficient. They were usually made of wood and shod with metal in places that received wear. Oxen pulled a two-furrow plow that had to be heavily leaned upon by the man guiding it to break up the clods.

At harvest time, the reapers cut the grain just below the ear with a sickle. Binders followed them to pick up the cut wheat heads, bind them into sheaves, and bind the weeds that were sorted out from the sheaves into separate bundles for burning. The sheaves of wheat were taken to the threshing floor in an ox-drawn cart.

The threshing floor was an open place on high ground that was open to the wind. It was hard-packed earth on level land about fifty feet square. It was probably shared, as not every farmer possessed such a place on his land. The wheat was placed on the ground, and a threshing machine called a *morag,* consisting of several rollers set in a frame, was rolled over the wheat. A contemporary model called a *noreg* is used in Egypt. The framework supports a seat for the driver. It has three parallel rollers, armed with metal disks.

The grain was winnowed by tossing it into the air so that the husks would be fanned away by the prevailing winds or the movement of a broad flat shovel. The grain was put through a sieve that retained any grit or pebbles while the grain fell through to be removed to the granaries and storehouses.

Each householder purchased small amounts and ground a day's supply into meal or flour. Every home had its mill—two hard round stones about eighteen inches in diameter placed one upon the other. A hole in the center of the top stone allowed the grain to pass through for grinding. An upright handle was attached to the top stone to turn it. This was a job for two women who faced each other. Each clasped the handle with one hand to rotate the stone. With the other hand, they fed grain into the hole. No wonder they ground just enough for a day's supply!

Bulgur

Bulgur is a staple food in the Near East. It is made of whole wheat kernels that have been cracked and cleaned. Because the wheat germ and bran are included, it is rich in nutrients. Used more and more in the United States recently, it may be found in markets next to the rice section or in health food stores.

Bulgur is wheat that is processed by a vigorous boiling of the grain for one half hour until the grain is three times its size. The cooked wheat is then spread on screens to cure in the sun. When the dried grain is crisp and brown, the hulls are sifted out and the wheat is ground into grades of extra-fine, fine, medium, and coarse.

When used as a breakfast cereal, slowly add one part bulgur to three parts boiling water and simmer on low heat covered for 20 minutes.

Add a cup uncooked bulgur to meat loaf or meat balls. It may be served for dinner with a vegetable according to the following recipe:

❧BULGUR WITH VEGETABLES

Ingredients	Utensils
Bulgur	Skillet
Eggplant	Wooden spoon
Onion	Paring knife
Parsley	Sauce pan
Butter	Measuring spoons
Salt	Measuring cups or metric
Celery (optional)	measuring containers
Carrots (optional)	
Cabbage (optional)	
Oil	

RECIPE

Standard	Metric
3 cups water	720 ml
1 cup bulgur	240 grams
1 eggplant	
1 onion, chopped	125 grams
1/2 cup chopped parsley	100 grams
2 tablespoons butter	30 grams
1 teaspoon salt	5 grams
1/4 cup oil	60 ml

Optional:
1/2 head chopped cabbage
1/2 bunch carrots, sliced
6 stalks celery, sliced

METHOD

Bring water to a boil. Add butter and salt. Slowly pour bulgur into boiling water. Cover and simmer slowly until almost all of the water is absorbed, about 20 minutes.

Place skillet on another burner on low heat. Heat the oil. Add eggplant that has been peeled and cut into 1-inch squares. Stir frequently with a wooden spoon. Add onions and cook until they are transparent but not brown. Celery, cabbage, and carrots are delicious when they are cooked in this manner. Cook until they are soft, with onions, if you wish, or they may be omitted. Add parsley to the mixture. Stir in the bulgur.

Serve in a vegetable dish.

Serves 6.

❧ KIBBI NAYYA / Ground Lamb with Bulgur

Kibbi Nayya may be cooked or served raw in the Near Eastern fashion with raw onions and Arab bread. (Arab bread recipe follows in the next chapter.)

Ingredients	Utensils
Ground lamb	Bowl
Bulgur	Colander
Salt	Skillet
Olive oil	Measuring spoons
Spices:	Measuring cups or metric
Nutmeg, allspice, pepper,	measuring containers
cayenne pepper, onion salt	

RECIPE

Standard	Metric
1/4 lb finely ground lamb	125 grams
1 cup bulgur	150 grams
1 teaspoon salt	5 grams
1/4 teaspoon of the following:	
Nutmeg, allspice, pepper,	
cayenne pepper, onion salt.	
1/2 cup olive oil	120 ml

METHOD

Place bulgur in a bowl. Add enough water to cover. Soak for 10 minutes. Drain the bulgur in a colander and blot as dry as you can with a paper towel. Place the soaked bulgur back in a dry bowl. Add ground lamb and seasonings. Blend well with your hands. Form into six 3-inch patties. If served raw, pour a small amount of the olive oil on each patty. If hot, fry in a skillet with the oil. Cook slowly on low heat, until meat is no longer red.

Serves 6.

❧CARROTS AND PEAS WITH SPICE

Ingredients	Utensils
Frozen peas	Skillet
Frozen carrots	Sauce pan
Parsley	Measuring spoons
Ginger	Blender
Turmeric	
Curry powder	
Mustard seeds	
Fenugreek seeds	
Oil	

RECIPE

Standard	Metric
1 package frozen peas (10 oz)	283 grams
1 package frozen carrots (10 oz)	283 grams
1/2 cup chopped parsley	125 grams
3 tablespoons vegetable oil or olive oil	45 ml
3–5 black mustard seeds	
3–5 whole fenugreek seeds	
Piece of ginger one inch long or 1 teaspoon ground ginger	5 grams
Small piece of turmeric or 1/2 teaspoon ground turmeric	3 grams
1 teaspoon curry powder	5 grams

or grind in a blender:
    6 whole peppercorn seeds
    2–3 whole cloves
    5 cumin seeds
    3 coriander seeds
    1 stick of cinnamon one inch long

METHOD

Heat oil in a skillet on medium heat. In it cook the mustard and fenugreek seeds until they pop. Add ginger and turmeric. Take skillet off the flame. Add 1/2 cup (120 ml) water that has been brought to the boiling point in a sauce pan. Add curry powder or ground spices and frozen carrots. Cook five minutes on medium heat. Turn to low heat. Add the frozen peas and cook the entire mixture for fifteen minutes.

Serve with bulgur.

Serves 4.

Matzo Meal Pancakes / *Jewish Passover*

All breads that are made with leaven (yeast, baking powder, soda, or sour dough) are prohibited for Jews throughout the world during the eight days of Passover, which begins in late March or early April. Passover, the Jewish Festival of Freedom, commemorates the hasty deliverance of the Israelites from their bondage in Egypt. God "passed over" Jewish homes when the firstborn died in Egypt. It was the custom in ancient days to bring a measure of grain to the Temple on the second day of Passover. The grain was an offering from the new spring harvest.

Consequently, matzos are eaten rather than ordinary bread. Matzos are specially prepared of flour and water under the supervision of a rabbi. Matzo meal is available in most supermarkets.

The following recipe makes a very light pancake that may be served with syrup or sprinkled with cinnamon and sugar. Unused pancakes may be cut into small pieces and added to soups for dumplings.

❧MATZO MEAL PANCAKES

Ingredients	*Utensils*
Matzo meal	Bowl
Eggs	Wire whisk
Oil for griddle	Rotary egg beater
Milk	Griddle
Water	Rubber spatula
Salt	Wooden spoon
	Pancake turner
	Measuring spoons
	Measuring cups or metric measuring containers

RECIPE

Standard	*Metric*
1/2 cup water	120 ml
1/2 cup milk	120 ml
1/2 cup matzo meal	50 grams
3 eggs, separated	
1 tablespoon oil	30 ml
Pinch of salt	2 grams

METHOD

Beat the egg yolks, salt, water, and milk in a bowl. Stir in the matzo meal with wooden spoon.

In another bowl, beat egg whites with a clean dry wire whisk, until the whites are stiff and stand in peaks. Fold the egg whites into the matzo meal batter with a rubber spatula. Refrigerate batter one half hour so that the flour absorbs the liquid.

Preheat skillet on medium heat. Grease with oil and a paper

towel. Pour 1/4 cup batter into skillet. Cook until bubbles form on top of the pancake. Turn and cook one minute on the other side. Remove with pancake turner. Serve with syrup or sugar and cinnamon.

Serves 4.

Challah

Challah is another traditional Jewish bread that is served on the Sabbath and special holidays. It is made of white wheat flour, then braided and baked in that form. It may be baked in a loaf or in small rolls.

Traditionally, two braided loaves are placed upon the table to symbolize the commandment given to Israel to keep the Sabbath. It is a reminder of the double portion of manna that was supplied to the Israelites for the Sabbath during their forty years wandering in the wilderness after their Exodus from Egypt.

Challah is a delicious bread to serve at any time.

CHALLAH / Jewish Sabbath Bread

Ingredients	*Utensils*
Yeast	Bowls
Sugar	Flour sifter
Salt	Cookie sheet
Eggs	Towel
Salad oil	Rotary beater
Flour (all-purpose)	Wooden spoon
Poppy seeds	Measuring spoons
	Measuring cups or metric
	measuring containers

RECIPE

Standard	Metric
4 1/3 cups all-purpose flour	607 grams
1 package dry yeast	7 grams
1 teaspoon salt	5 grams
2 tablespoons sugar	30 grams
2 well-beaten eggs	
2 tablespoons salad oil	30 ml
1 1/4 cups lukewarm water	300 ml
1 egg yolk	
1 teaspoon poppy seeds	8 grams

METHOD

Place yeast in small bowl. Add sugar. Add 1/4 cup warm water. (Water should be the same temperature as your finger.) Let mixture stand for five minutes.

Sift the flour into a large bowl. Add salt. Make a well in the center of flour. Add the well-beaten eggs, 1 cup water, oil, and yeast mixture. Stir with wooden spoon until all of the flour has been worked into the dough.

Place on floured counter and knead for 10 minutes. When it is time to stop, the dough will be shiny, smooth, and elastic.

Rub a little oil on the surface of the dough. Place in large bowl and put in a warm spot to rise. When double in size (about 1 hour), punch it down, knead a few times, then let it rise until it's twice its size once more.

Divide dough into three equal rolls about one inch wide and six to eight inches long. On a cookie sheet, braid the three pieces together. Let rise again. Brush a little egg yolk on the surface and scatter poppy seeds over the dough.

Preheat oven to 375° F (or 191° C). Bake for 50 minutes.

Serves 12.

Egyptian Dynasty XVIII. Wall painting from the tomb of Nakht, Thebes.
Photograph by Egyptian Expedition, The Metropolitan Museum of Art.

❧3❧
Bread and Couscous

The Egyptians grew the finest wheat in the ancient world, although they very likely received the idea of farming from the Mesopotamians, who had been cultivating their lands for over a thousand years. However, the Egyptians had two natural advantages. First, they were protected by hot deserts on the east and west, a sea on the north, and a river with dangerous rapids high in the south. They were not prey to invaders as were the people who lived on the Tigris and Euphrates rivers. Second, the Nile River regularly overflowed over a large area beyond its banks. Each year the land was renewed with exceedingly rich silt washed down from the highlands. The canals did not have to be as long and complicated as those in Mesopotamia, nor did the soil have a tendency to become saline (too salty) because of the evaporation of irrigation water. The Egyptians harnessed the yearly flooding of the Nile efficiently. Wheat became the most important crop in the world, and the men who controlled its growth became wealthy and powerful.

The Egyptians were equally efficient as recorders of their daily life. Paintings on temples and tombs reveal the way they dressed, their furniture, their contacts with other nations, and their farming methods and cookery. We may see them plowing the ground with a plow pulled by two oxen and guided by a man. A sickle was replaced by a scythe with a longer handle and a sharper blade to harvest the grain. Some used a cradle. It had a wooden frame that ran parallel to the blade so that the stalks fell together on the frame when they were cut. But it was a very heavy tool, and it required a great deal of strength to use it.

After the grain was cut, it was beaten with flails. They were sticks with loose strips hinged to the center stick with pieces of leather. Next, the kernels were tossed in the air with pitchforks so that the wind could blow away the dry bits of chaff that were still clinging to the grain. Almost the same procedure was followed thereafter until Cyrus McCormick invented the reaper in the United States in 1830.

The Egyptians believed in a kind of immortality. They placed food in the tombs of the deceased to ensure them enough for the "other life." Wheat, barley, bread, porridge, quail, beef ribs, figs, berries, and wine were provided for kings and queens. "Pharaoh's wheat" has been found in the tombs of kings that is as fine as that grown today. The peasants did not fare so well. They, and the slaves who built the pyramids, were given only flatbread and onions.

Other pictures show men doing the cooking. They used a kind of charcoal brazier. Women ground the grain on stone querns. Flatbreads were baked in clay ovens shaped like cones. Dough was stored in jars near the ovens. One day an interesting change occurred in the dough in one of the jars. It grew!

Imagine the surprise of the Egyptian servant when he found the puffy dough! He baked it anyway and found it to be lighter than the ordinary flatbread that he was accustomed to baking. He did not know that there is a tiny plant in the air, called yeast, that had settled on the dough. Wheat is the only grain that contains a substance known as gluten. Yeast combines with the natural sugar within the dough to form a gas that makes bubbles. Because the gluten stretches, the bubbles are

Egyptian Dynasty XI (Funerary model of a granary shop from the tomb of Meket-Rē, Thebes.
The Metropolitan Museum of Art, Museum Excavations, 1919-1920, Rogers Fund, supplemented by contributions of Edward S. Harkness.

held within the dough. You may sometimes hear a few pops when you knead the dough. The gas dissipates when the bread is baked, but the expanded shape remains.

The servant had saved a little bit of the puffy dough in order to add it to some dough in another jar close to the oven. It, too, became puffy. Thus, the first bakers of bread began in Egypt. It was very well regarded—Egyptians were content to receive it as their wages. The terms "dough" and "bread-winner" are to be taken literally.

Not everyone began eating round loaves of risen white bread. They were only for kings, queens, and priests. At least forty types were baked: some round, some braided, some baked with milk and eggs. Eggs made the flat bread lighter, just like a pancake. Some were even sweetened with honey. Most of the populace ate ordinary flatbread, however.

So much wheat was grown that the Egyptians became world traders. Trade routes had already been established to India and through the mountain passes of Europe. Ships from Crete, an island near Greece that may have been settled by people from Mesopotamia, and ships from Phoenicia, present-day Lebanon, carried wheat to ports on the Mediterranean Sea as far as Spain and even to Britain, in return for the tin that was needed to make utensils of bronze. Greece was to prove a ready market, as the people there were to need large amounts of cereals. Barges from Egypt found their way to the land of Punt in East Africa. Punt is believed to be present-day Ethiopia.

As the centuries passed, Egypt was replaced by other empires as a world power, but its identity and name have survived throughout the ages. It is a republic today whose borders extend from the Red Sea westward some 700 miles into the desert beyond the Nile Valley. Although its capital, Cairo, is a modern, heavily populated city, most of the people live on the small farms along the banks of the Nile. Most of them work in the fields and live as the ancients have lived through thousands of years. Now a huge dam, the Aswan Dam, controls the flood waters and releases water as it is needed into canals. Two and three crops are produced a year where only one was produced formerly, but in some places the farmers water their fields by hand, raising water from the Nile with the ancient *shadoof,* a water lift with a bucket on one end.

Cotton and wheat are the chief products, but not enough wheat is grown to sustain the populace and some must be imported. A new type of wheat has been introduced recently. It is a short-stemmed grain that was developed in America, and in 1960, it doubled the production when used in India and Pakistan. The Egyptian peasant, who cultivates his two acres as carefully as a gardener, shuns anything that is mechanical and modern and he complains about the new wheat. The bakers in Cairo and housewives protest that it makes tough bread, but with the new wheat seeds, production has risen to 100,000 tons per year.

In addition to their fondness for bread, Egyptians eat large amounts of vegetables, and pigeons stuffed with crushed wheat. There are enough birds to meet the heaviest demand. A nourishing bean and lentil dish called *ful* is served every day. It is sold on the streets and in good restaurants. Because it is cheap, it is called "the poor man's meat." The beans and lentils should be boiled long and slowly.

Between Egypt and Mesopotamia, a large peninsula borders the Red Sea on the west and the Persian Gulf on the east. It is known as the Arabian peninsula. Waves of people poured out from this area at various times to settle in Mesopotamia and the surrounding area. Most of them were nomads, traveling on the backs of camels and living off their herds. They were to control much of the overland trade to India. They brought pepper, spices, the bitter orange, and sugar to the Near East. One of the young men of Mecca in southern Arabia, Mohammed by name, became a prophet-leader of most of Arabia six hundred years after the birth of Jesus. He founded a religion that was accepted by most of the people in North Africa. They are called Moslems. They do not eat pork, but enjoy fabulous fruits, lamb, and a dish called *couscous* made of hard wheat. It is the national dish of Morocco and is quite tasty if it is cooked correctly.

The Arabs have a reverence for bread and water. Wherever they settled they improved the methods of irrigation. Tinkling fountains grace the courtyards of their buildings. Some of them live quite differently than we do—especially the nomads traveling with their flocks. They are considered to be a hospitable people. Wealthy sheiks have been known to entertain foreign visitors with lavish feasts.

On the other side of the Red Sea, south of Egypt, is another very ancient country—Ethiopia. Ethiopia was one of the first nations to be converted to the Christian religion. Almost as old as Egypt, it was ancient before the time of Jesus.

A steeply climbing highway leads one through rich and fertile land to reach a capital city that has modern and beautiful buildings. The open air market in Addis Ababa is huge with many foods on display. Coffee is native to Ethiopia. A great deal of wheat and millet are grown as well as citrus fruits and vegetables of all kinds. Several types of bread are on display. The most common is called *injera*, and it is prepared in a special large pan with a cover as it was thousands of years ago from a type of millet called *tef*.

Millet is a cousin of wheat. It is just as nutritious although the seeds are much smaller than the kernels of wheat. It is grown in large quantities in Central Africa where there are areas not favorable to wheat cultivation. The soil is prepared in the same way. It prefers warm climates. The people in Eastern Europe and Asia also use it for bread making and cake baking. It was one of the royal cereals in ancient China. It is not used for human consumption in the United States, but a type of millet is grown here for feeding livestock.

We will have to do a little bit of improvising in order to make *injera, couscous,* and the Arab bread of Africa, but they are really fun to try.

Arab Bread

Bread is sacred to an Arab because it is a symbol of life to him. Arabs believe that Allah, their name for God, sent grain from heaven, and it should never be wasted or treated with disdain.

If a piece of bread is found on the street, it is touched to the lips and given to a stray dog.

Bread often serves as a plate with the other food placed upon it, or, as in Iraq, it may be stuffed with meat.

Arab bread is well-suited for stuffing because a large space appears in the center after it is baked.

❧ARAB POCKET BREAD

Ingredients	Utensils
Dry yeast	Flour sifter
Sugar	Small and large bowls
Salt	Cookie sheet
Flour (all-purpose)	Wooden spoon
Olive oil	Rolling pin
Warm water	Measuring spoons
	Measuring cups or metric measuring containers

RECIPE

Standard	Metric
1 package dry yeast	7 grams
1 teaspoon sugar	5 grams
1 teaspoon salt	5 grams
3 cups sifted flour	384 grams
1 tablespoon olive oil	15 ml
1 1/4 cups warm water	300 ml

METHOD

Dissolve yeast in small bowl filled with one half of the water. Add sugar.

Sift flour and salt into a large bowl. Pour in oil, yeast water, and remaining water and stir well with wooden spoon until the dough holds together. Turn out on a floured counter and knead for 10 minutes.

Place dough back in the bowl, spread a little oil on the surface, cover with a towel, and place in a warm place to double in size, about one and one half hours.

Take risen dough out of the bowl and knead again two or three times. Divide dough into six round balls. Roll each ball with the rolling pin on the floured counter until it is flat and six inches in diameter.

Bake in preheated oven 500° F (260° C) on ungreased cookie sheet placed on rack in lowest position in the oven. Bake three minutes. It should puff in the center. Turn each bread over and bake three more minutes on the other side.

Butter surface of each bread as soon as it is removed from the oven. Cover with a towel while they cool.

They may be eaten warm or cool.

Yield: 6.

Injera from Ethiopia

Nowhere else in the world were as many varieties of millet developed as in Ethiopia. *Tef*, a very high grade millet flour, is used to make a type of bread called *injera* that is like a giant pancake.

Baked on a special griddle with a lid, it is made of flour and water that has been kept in a warm place for two or three days. The result is a bubbly fermented batter that produces a slightly sour taste. It is a good accompaniment to the hot, highly seasoned food that Ethiopians enjoy. They use the flat-bread as a dip or sop for the liquids that surround their meat dishes, as the people of India also use it.

Millet flour may be purchased at most health food or specialty stores. It will turn sour if mixed with water and kept for a few days, but the same taste may be achieved with a pancake mix and club soda, obtainable at any supermarket.

A cast iron skillet or crepe pan and any lid that fits will suffice. An injera is fun to make.

⚜INJERA

Ingredients	Utensils
Pancake mix	Skillet with lid to fit
Flour (all-purpose)	Rubber spatula
Club soda	Ladle
Water	Bowl
Shortening or oil	Rotary beater or wooden spoon
	Measuring spoons
	Measuring cups or metric measuring containers

RECIPE

Standard	Metric
1 1/2 cups pancake mix	180 grams
3 tablespoons flour	45 grams
1 cup water	240 ml
1 1/2 cups club soda	360 ml
1 tablespoon oil for skillet	15 ml

METHOD

With a beater or spoon, mix all the ingredients together in a bowl. The batter will be thin.

Preheat the griddle on medium heat until a drop of water will bounce when dropped upon it. Lightly grease the skillet.

Remove the skillet from heat. Pour 1/3 of a ladle full of batter on skillet. Roll it around until the batter makes a thin coating on the pan. Pour any excess into a bowl.

Return to heat and bake one minute with a lid over the skillet. Use a pot holder to remove lid and be careful as steam will escape.

Remove the injera onto a plate with rubber spatula. It is easily removed. Repeat the process and serve in a basket or on a platter.

Good with a highly seasoned dish.

Serves 6.

Couscous

Couscous is a very old and special dish of North Africa made of coarsely ground hard wheat called semolina or millet flour. Although couscous from Africa may be found in specialty food stores and in some supermarkets, farina or cream of wheat may be used.

It probably received its name from the way it is cooked. It is steamed, and as the steam escapes through the holes of the couscous bowl, it makes a coosh-coosh sound. Although Moroccans have a special utensil for cooking couscous, we can substitute a pan of boiling water, a colander, and a towel. Some people possess double boilers with vegetable steamer attachments. That will be an excellent substitute.

Traditionally, the diners in an Arab meal sit cross-legged in a circle around the serving bowl, placed on a low table. Each person eats with a spoon of wood held in the right hand. They eat from the outer edges of the bowl, leaving the blessing of Allah for the center. After the couscous, a bowl of milk is passed around to each person, and they follow that with strong coffee.

❧COUSCOUS

Ingredients
Couscous or cream of wheat
Butter
Salt
Water

Utensils
Colander
Sauce pan large enough to
  hold colander
Cheesecloth or strong paper
  towel
Bowl
Plate
Measuring spoons
Measuring cups or metric
  measuring containers

RECIPE

Standard	Metric
4 1/2 cups boiling water	1 1/25 liter
4 cups couscous	500 grams
6 tablespoons butter	100 grams
2 tablespoons oil	30 ml
Salt and pepper to taste	
1 cup lukewarm water	240 ml

METHOD
Moisten the crushed grain and place it on cheesecloth in a steamer or colander. Place a towel between the steamer and the sauce pan of boiling water. Steam uncovered for 40 minutes. Remove from heat and turn out on a large plate and work out any lumps that have formed. Use a fork or your fingers.

Add salt and pepper. Work in the oil and the lukewarm water. Leave for 15 minutes. Return to colander. Place over boiling water to steam for 15 more minutes. Turn onto serving dish and add the butter.

Serves 4.

❧COUSCOUS TAGINE

Ingredients
Couscous
Onions
Carrots
Peas
Green pepper
Lamb shoulder
Frying chicken
Tomatoes
Pepper
Salt
Spices:
   Bouquet garni, cloves,
   cinnamon, celery salt,
   cumin

Utensils
Sauce pan
Colander
Knife
Skillet
Measuring spoons
Measuring cups or metric
   measuring containers
Large serving platter

RECIPE

Standard	Metric
2 small onions	250 grams
1 bunch sliced carrots or	283 grams
1 package (10 oz) frozen	
sliced carrots	
1/2 green pepper, sliced	125 grams
1 cup canned tomatoes	240 ml
1 cup peas	240 ml
1 lb lamb shoulder	500 grams
2–3 lb frying chicken cut	1000–1500 grams
into pieces	
Dash of salt, pepper, and not	
more than 1/4 teaspoon of	
cloves, bouquet garni,	
cinnamon, cumin, and celery	
salt	
4 cups couscous	500 grams
3 cups water	720 ml

METHOD

Sauté all of the ingredients except frozen peas and tomatoes until lightly browned. Add tomatoes and spices. Place the meat and vegetables in a sauce pan. Add three cups of water. Place colander with couscous in it over vegetables and broth and steam uncovered for 50 minutes. Peas may be added for the last 5 minutes.

To serve, place couscous in the center of the platter. Make a well in it for the broth. Arrange meat and vegetables around the couscous.

Serves 6.

Athenian krater (vase) c. 440 B.C. depicts The Return of Persephone: Persephone rises from the earth in the presence of Hermes, Hecate, and Demeter. Attributed to the "Persephone painter."

The Metropolitan Museum of Art, Fletcher Fund, 1928.

❧4❧
Epicurus and Apicius

Greece, a mountainous peninsula that basks in the sunshine on the northern side of the Mediterranean Sea, is deeply indented with countless bays and inlets. Its rocky shores make it an ideal spot for fishermen and sailors, but its mountains and sparse soil do not favor the farmer. Yet agricultural communities nestled between the mountains as early as 6500 B.C. At one time, the Mycenaeans from the mainland conquered the fertile isle of Crete. They built the city of Troy immortalized by the epics of Homer. Later, about 1200 B.C., they succumbed to a people from the vast steppes of Eurasia who were called Dorians. They were a branch of the Indo-Europeans who were to swoop down on many areas of the continent, including Italy, Turkey, Persia (now called Iran), and India. Although they were nomads, they were acquainted with grain culture. Once they arrived in Greece, an era of primitive farming began in the foothills and on the plains. Civilization was retarded for a time, but it was to become one of the most highly developed cultures of the ancient world. The Greeks created a kind of democracy, and their art and architecture, drama, and philosophy have never been surpassed. For the first time, cookery was considered a fine art.

Originally, the land was forested and abundant with wild game. Achilles and his contemporaries dined on roasted meat.

Cypriot terracottas, 1000-600 B.C. Statuette group: Two women grinding and winnowing corn. *The Metropolitan Museum of Art, the Cesnola Collection; purchased by subscription, 1874–76.*

When the population was scarce, there was enough fertile soil in the foothills and plains to grow enough wheat and barley for every family, although only twelve bushels per acre were harvested every other April or May. The land was allowed to rest every other year. A wooden plow barely scratched the earth's surface before the autumn rains. The softened earth was plowed once more and the seeds were sown to sprout in the spring. Olives and vineyards were more profitable for the farmers. Honey, the only sweetener, was produced in abundance by the bees who feasted on wild flowers and clover on Mt. Hymettus.

It did not take long for the valleys that were separated from one another by high, impassable mountains to become overpopulated. Gradually the sea beckoned; it was never more than fifty miles away at any point. Ships were built, and olives were traded for wheat from Egypt or from the Scythians who cultivated grain on the northern shores of the Black Sea.

The forests were denuded when ships were built. Since there were no roots to hold the soil together or falling leaves to restore its fertility, it was washed away. The few remaining trees were sacrificed for the olive tree. Its deep roots drain the soil, but it gave a few Greeks great wealth. Olive oil was in great demand for medicine, soap, lighting, and cooking. It became a medium of exchange and new city-states were established in ports throughout the Mediterranean Sea. Lisbon in Portugal was a Greek colony. Another was Massilia (Marseilles, France). There were many others in Sicily and along the eastern Mediterranean as well as the Black Sea. Byzantium was an important port near the old city of Troy. Most of the Greeks dined simply despite the wealth that many gained. Excess was not encouraged. Plato, the philosopher, preached moderation and temperance. In *The Republic*, he states his idea of the healthy life. "As for nourishment, men will, no doubt, make themselves flour, either from wheat or barley which they will knead or cook on a griddle." He called griddle cakes "noble cakes." Athenian cooks possessed the same type of griddles, frying pans, pots for boiling, ladles, etc., that we do. They were made of copper or iron.

Another Greek philosopher, Epicurus, conducted a school in his garden near Athens. Because he taught that happiness was the result of pleasure, he has mistakenly been labeled a slave to appetite, but he really advocated moderation and temperance in the choice of those things that bring pleasure. Indeed, he lived upon the food that he grew in his small field, declaring that barley cakes and water were enough for his daily needs. The word *epicure* that is derived from his name is often used to describe a person who likes fine food, perfectly prepared and attractively served—one who displays fastidiousness in his tastes.

The same type of fastidiousness in taste is evident in the perfectly proportioned public buildings and temples of Athens. It is rather strange that most of the homes were not as exquisite. Kitchens were inadequate, as there was no outlet for smoke. Therefore, most of the cooking was done in a small courtyard on a charcoal stove, weather permitting. Athenians enjoyed outdoor living underneath their sunny skies. It was a common sight to see groups of men hiking to a grassy spot beyond the city walls carrying a basket containing a carefully prepared supper. Women were not included in the picnic as they rarely left the confines of their homes, but they tried to outdo one another in the preparation of the basket supper. These suppers included olives, dried figs and dates, perhaps an apple or pear, some radishes or onions, and fancy pastries filled with cheese or honey. Flatbreads were used as plates for bite-sized pieces of fried sole, steamed bass with mulberry sauce, or baked turbot.

Breakfast and luncheon were generally simple, but dinner at sunset could be lavish if guests were invited. Five men was the favorite number for parties. They reclined upon couches placed around the table. Men were serious cooks; they were highly regarded and well paid. Food became a fascinating subject for discourse and literature. As many as twenty cookbooks were mentioned by Athenaeus in his treatise on food and feasting.

Recipes were often included in plays to the delight of the audience who assembled in outdoor theaters. The seats of the theater were arranged in a semicircle on the side of a hill. They were stone terraces that rose in rows above a circle or dancing place that was called the orchestra. In some theaters, the orchestra had originally been a threshing floor that was marked out by circling cattle as they trampled the grain under their hooves.

Public bakeries were the pride of Athenians. Several types of bread and cakes as well as bushels of unground wheat were sold at the *agora* (market place). Most of the bread was flat—the risen loaves of yeast bread were only available for feast days. Often a well-beaten egg was introduced as a leavening agent in Athens as every family was able to own one chicken.

The men of the family who marketed at the *agora* could also buy lentil soup, hot porridge, cheese, figs, olives, milk, and wine. Meat was expensive. Only in times of plenty was it available, chopped and spiced and wrapped in grape leaves. It was steamed in a skillet. Seafood was always plentiful.

Roman Statuettes, c. 25 B.C. — c. 200 A.D. Farmyard group, bronze. *The Metropolitan Museum of Art, Rogers Fund, 1909.*

The Spartans in the Peloponnesus, south of Athens, had a cuisine that made the poor Athenian who could only afford a porridge of barley shudder. Pork stock, salt, and vinegar may have made hardy men, but the combination is too awful to contemplate. And the Athenians liked to contemplate and discuss food. They enjoyed talking and writing about it almost as much as eating it.

With the Romans, it was a different story. They simply liked to eat! There were big spenders in Rome who dined with an unparalleled opulence — too much — too often — and too expensively. In the beginning of their history, their wants had

49

been simple. Bread, porridge, green vegetables, and a little pork were sufficient. Italy was an early melting pot of many Indo-European tribes who came from central Europe at various times. Historians do not agree on the origin of the Etruscans who lived in the fertile areas in the north of Italy. Some claim they are of Near Eastern origin. Eventually the Latins who lived on the Tiber River controlled the whole peninsula, the Grecian southern area as well as the north. Latin Rome was to become the largest empire of the ancient world—the whole Mediterranean Sea area and all of Europe west of the Rhine and south of the Danube rivers. The largest food supply since the beginnings of civilization was theirs.

From Egypt, they took the wheat that was basic to their diet. One third of the Roman population received free grain from huge storehouses in the city. It has been said that the Roman soldier conquered the world on pancakes and *puls,* a type of grain paste.

Those that were more prosperous delighted in fruit for dessert. They might have Persian peaches, Armenian apricots, or dates from Mesopotamia. From Spain, they could have more wine, olive oil, and rabbits. (They called Spain *Hispania,* the Latin word for rabbit.) Pork has a pleasant taste after it has been cured, and it keeps without refrigeration. This, from Gaul (France and Germany), was a favorite. They paid dearly for the spices from India. The Arabs kept the sources of spices a secret. Those who could afford it enjoyed shellfish that had been brought inland at great expense, either by slave labor, or by specially built canals directly to their villas. Asparagus, broccoli, cabbages, and cucumbers accompanied exotic fish and meat preparations that we would consider very unappetizing. They were served with strange and heavily spiced sauces.

A wealthy Roman, Apicius, wrote a book on cookery. He collected recipes from the Greeks and spent lavish sums of money in search of a new food or new manner of preparing

A summer repast at the home of Lucullus at Tusculum c. 261 B.C. by Gustave Boulanger. From Earl Shinn, *The Chefs D'Oeuvre D'Art of International Exhibition*, 1878, ed. by Edward Strahan. *New York Public Library, Picture Collection.*

foods. He did develop a recipe for pancakes that is quite similar to any found in a modern cookbook. The difference is in the syrup he recommended—honey and pepper! Unfortunately, Apicius was not satisfied with such simple fare. One day, he gave an elaborate banquet. At the height of the feast, he slipped outside his villa and quietly committed suicide. Poor man! He had squandered so much money on food that he had only the equivalent of half a million dollars left. He chose to die rather than live the rest of his life in a more frugal manner. Monks who lived during the Middle Ages copied his cookbook and it was translated into many languages. Recipes for the sauces and many other items are included as well as the pancake recipe.

Although most of the wealthy lived in beautiful villas, too many of the Romans were forced to make crowded tenements their homes. They were seven or eight stories high. Water had to be fetched from street fountains. Cooking facilities were poor. A bit of grain or lentil porridge washed down with vinegar, and a bit of salt fish for dinner was the best the poor city dweller could afford. They were sometimes given free bread as well as free grain.

Agricultural methods did not make an outstanding advance in Roman times. The hand-guided plow remained in the field. However, the saddle quern of Egypt and Mesopotamia was replaced by a grinding stone attached to a lever. It ground the grain on another stone with a side-to-side motion, rather than backwards and forwards by hand. Next, a donkey was attached to a longer lever. As he trudged around and around, the grain was ground more rapidly between two large stones. Then water wheels upon streams were employed to move the heavy grinding stones even more efficiently. The miller became a power in the community. He was also the baker. He would have felt quite at home in the mills that are still being used in some rural villages in the United States.

The practical Romans solved the problem of irrigation in a marvelous manner. Huge aqueducts of stone carried water long distances. Several are still standing and are in use in Europe. One in Segovia, Spain, built of perfectly chiseled stones, stands high above the town. It is quite an inspiring sight. Such aqueducts transferred many tons of water to soil where plants could not otherwise have survived.

While Greece generally looked toward the east, Rome eyed the west as well. They had cities in Britain and built fine homes and roads in Spain. There, the cultivation of wheat for the expanding empire, as well as the olive and vine, was very productive. The Phoenicians had already planted the popular

Mill and bakery at Pompeii from *Museum of Antiquity;* A Description of
Ancient Life by L.W. Yaggy and T.F. Haines. *New York Public Library,*
Picture Collection.

garbanzo bean. The Romans may have had some knowledge of
the bitter orange from India, but it was not until several centuries later that the sweet orange from China grew successfully in Spain.

Yearly, great grain fleets sailed from North Africa and Spain.
A route was discovered to India to purchase the precious
spices that were a very important addition to the Roman cuisine. Historians have commented on the unusual preference of
the Romans for too much seasoning in their food. Too much—
that seems to have been a part of their story. Too much land to
govern, too much poverty for the masses, too much self-indul-
gence on the part of the wealthy.

It will be noted when we study the cuisine of modern Italy that it does not resemble the cooking of imperial Rome. The food is seasoned, but with delicacy and subtlety, to enhance the natural flavor of each dish. Each bite that one has of chicken or fish seems better than the last. The vegetables taste as though they were just plucked out of the garden and cooked minutes before serving. Fruits are displayed in many attractive ways.

The Roman empire was divided into two sectors in 309 A.D. It had finally adopted Christianity, although each sector had a slightly different form. Greece became a part of the eastern section, the Byzantine empire, with a capital at Constantinople, the old Greek port of Byzantium. It was in this area that the emblem of the master chef, a tall, white pleated hat, became recognized as a reward for outstanding skill in culinary achievement. It seems that there were many scholars who liked to cook as well as study. When they were oppressed by the authorities, probably for their independent way of thinking, they sought refuge in monasteries. The priests of the Greek Orthodox church wore and still wear a tall, pleated, black hat. The men came to the monasteries disguised as priests. However, some of them felt it was not really honest to wear a priest's hat. They wore the same type—but it was white. Because of their skill as cooks, the hat gradually became a hat worn only by a master chef.

The empires of Greece and Rome extended many new ideas to parts of Europe and Asia. Although farming began in Mesopotamia and Egypt, soldiers and colonists from Greece and Rome took it into areas it might not have reached otherwise for a long time.

The word *cereal*, used to describe the grains that are the basis of the human diet, has been borrowed from the Romans. Ceres was the name of the goddess of agriculture. (The Greeks called her Demeter.) Both the Greeks and the Romans explained the

54

changes from summer to winter by means of the following myth:

Ceres had to sow seeds in the spring, tend them and bless the harvest in the autumn. She also helped her daughter Proserpina (Persephone, Gr.) with her task of tending the flowers. For these reasons, she chose to live on earth rather than upon Mt. Olympus, with the other deities.

One day while Proserpina was busy with her flowers on the Isle of Sicily, the earth opened up and out came Pluto, god of the underworld, in a chariot. Before she could cry out for help, Proserpina had been abducted to his underworld palace, where she was very unhappy. Ceres, grief stricken over her loss, asked the world to help her but it would not. In her despair, she neglected her duties of seeding and harvesting and famine resulted. At last the Fates stepped in and ruled that Proserpina might live with her mother six months of the year but the other six months had to be spent in Pluto's underground palace. Spring came once again when Proserpina and Ceres were reunited, and the seeds sprouted and flowers blossomed. But at the end of six months, Proserpina went back to her underground home and the barren winter began.

The following dessert is made from a cereal, farina or cream of wheat.

❧HALVA

Ingredients	Utensils
Cream of wheat	Bowl
Butter	Wooden spoon
Sugar	Rotary egg beater
Egg	Sauce pan
Honey	9-in-square pan
Cinnamon	Measuring spoons
Almonds	Measuring cups or metric
Water	measuring containers

RECIPE

Standard	Metric
1/4 cup butter	60 grams
1/2 cup sugar	120 grams
1 egg	
1/2 cup cream of wheat	120 grams
1/4 cup almonds (ground)	60 grams
1/4 teaspoon cinnamon	2 grams

SYRUP

1/2 cup honey	120 ml
1/4 cup water	60 ml

METHOD

Place butter in a bowl to soften at room temperature. Cream in sugar with a wooden spoon until butter and sugar are light and fluffy and the color of cream. Add egg. Beat well. Add cream of wheat, cinnamon, and almonds. Pour into a greased square cake pan. Bake 35 minutes at 350° F (177° C).

While the cake is baking, boil the honey and water in a sauce pan for five minutes.

Pour over baked halva. Let it cool in cake pan. Cut into squares when cool and place squares on a plate for serving.

Serves 6–8.

KOURABIEDES

A Greek cookie served at festivals and special occasions.

Ingredients	Utensils
Butter	Large bowl
Sugar	Flour sifter
Egg	Wooden spoon
Flour (all-purpose)	Cookie sheet
Baking powder	Fork

Ground cloves
Salt
Powdered sugar
Chopped almonds

Cooling rack
Measuring spoons
Measuring cups or metric
   measuring containers

Standard	*Metric*
1/2 cup soft butter	120 grams
1/2 cup sugar	120 grams
1 egg yolk	
1 cup sifted flour	128 grams
1 teaspoon baking powder	5 grams
1/2 teaspoon ground cloves	3 grams
1/2 teaspoon salt	3 grams
1/4 cup chopped almonds	40 grams
1/2 cup powdered sugar	35 grams
1 teaspoon vanilla	5 ml

METHOD

In a large bowl, cream butter and sugar with a wooden spoon until they are light and fluffy. Add the egg yolk, vanilla, and stir.

Sift flour, measure one cup. Resift into bowl with egg mixture, flour, salt, and baking powder. Add almonds and cloves. The dough will be stiff. Mix well with your hands or wooden spoon.

Refrigerate, covered, for one hour.

Shape into one-inch balls. Place on greased cookie sheet about one inch apart. Flatten each cookie with a fork.

Bake in preheated oven 350° F (177° C) 20 minutes, until cookies are light and golden.

While cookies are warm, sprinkle a little powdered sugar on each. Cool on wire rack.

Yield: 3 dozen cookies.

Phyllo Leaves

Phyllo (filo) leaves are used in many Greek recipes. They are made of white wheat flour, water, salt, and a little olive oil and carefully kneaded and stretched on a table until the dough is as thin as tissue paper. They may be purchased in specialty food shops. Sometimes strudel leaves, which are similar, are available in the frozen food sections of markets. They may be used equally well. The leaves should be covered until they are ready to use. Brush them with butter immediately after uncovering. They may be frozen until further use. Always let them thaw slowly at room temperature.

SPANAKOPITA / Greek Spinach Pie

Ingredients	Utensils
Phyllo (filo) leaves	Colander
Butter	Small sauce pan
Frozen spinach	Knife
Feta cheese (a Greek cheese)	Rotary egg beater
Cottage cheese	Whisk
Eggs	Skillet
Onion	Square 9-inch cake pan
Salt and pepper	Wooden spoon
Dried dill (optional)	

RECIPE

Standard	Metric
1/2 lb phyllo leaves (about 12)	
1/4 cup butter	60 grams
2 packages frozen spinach (10 oz each)	565 grams
1/4 lb feta cheese	100 grams
1/4 lb cottage cheese	100 grams
3 eggs, separated	

58

1 small onion	125 grams
2 tablespoons dried dill (optional)	30 grams
Salt and pepper to taste	

METHOD

Drain the thawed spinach in a colander until almost all of the liquid is removed. Press down with wooden spoon to press out as much as you can.

Beat the egg yolks with rotary beater. Break cheese into small pieces and add to eggs. Sauté onions and spinach in a skillet. Add to egg and cheese. Add seasoning.

Beat egg whites in a clean bowl with dry wire whisk until they are stiff and stand in peaks. Fold them into mixture with wooden spoon.

Grease cake pan. Spread six buttered phyllo sheets on bottom of pan. Cut to fit. Spread spinach mixture over phyllo sheets. Cover with remaining phyllo sheets.

Bake in oven preheated to 350° F (177° C) for one hour.

Cut in squares and serve.

Serves 6.

❧5❧
Cowboys vs. Settlers of Eurasia

Shish kebab or gulyas, buttermilk or dried milk, yoghurt or cheese, day after day, month after month, year after year. That was the only food of the horsemen and women who spent most of their lives in the saddle riding fierce ponies across the vast steppes or plains of Eurasia. At the same time that people in Mesopotamia, Egypt, India, and China were cultivating grain and building cities, tribes of nomads who have been named Indo-Europeans were herding their flocks into good pasture land or fighting one another with bows and arrows in eastern Europe and Asia.

They probably started out in an area near the Caspian Sea and then spread out over the steppes in every direction. They moved with the seasons, guiding their herds over the vast plains. Winters were long and severe, yet their homes were merely covered wagons made of goat skins and mounted on wheels so that teams of oxen could easily pull them. Clay replicas of their wagons have been unearthed in Hungary. They left only meager records of themselves since people on the move do not spend time writing books or building monuments.

Nor was eating or cooking of much concern to them. They simply milked their cows or mares, carried the milk in pouches made of the lining of cows' stomachs, and ate the cheese that was formed beside the saddle on a day's journey.

The Devastating Onslaught of the Plundering Magyars: desolation of the
district of Theiss and Danube, end of IX Century.
From *Harmsworth History of the World,* London, 1914. *New York Public
Library, Picture Collection.*

A substance called rennet in the stomach lining turned the
milk to cheese. Sometimes they boiled the milk and let it dry
in the sun. Dried milk is easy to carry in the saddle. If they
had no milk, they drank the blood of their horses by carefully
cutting a vein. It really seems gruesome, but did not harm the
pony.

Whenever they had time to stop at a campfire, they strung
pieces of meat along swords and broiled them over the campfire. Shish kebab is similarly served with flourish in many restaurants today. They also cooked the meat with onions in a
kettle hung over the fire to make the gulyas of Hungary.

They did not bother to spend time growing grain or vegetables. Instead they plundered the storehouses of settlers who
may have come from the Middle East or the Slavs, other Indo-

61

European tribes who preferred to till the soil. After discovering that their beloved ponies became larger and stronger on a diet of oats and hay, they might settle long enough to grow a few crops, providing they were able to defend themselves from the other nomads who rushed upon them at a moment's notice and fled as swiftly, leaving death and starvation in their wake. Whenever a tribe of people nudged others out of the way, the whole plain would reverberate as each group fought for new pasture land until the strongest prevailed.

All of the Indo-European tribes spoke languages that contained similar words—especially important terms for mother, father, or the names for animals and trees. The Slavs and Aryans who eventually settled in the east were also related to the Dorians, Latins and Saxons, Franks, Celts, and Germanic tribes near the Danube and Rhine rivers. There were other nomadic tribes whose language was not at all related—the Huns, Magyars, and later the Turks and Mongols. However, all had one purpose in common—to find the best pasture land for their herds, the measure of their wealth.

As we have noticed in the case of the Dorians and Latins, high mountain passes did not prevent them from gaining their objective. They crossed the Alps to conquer Greece and Italy and no longer roamed. After years of farming, they built cities and empires. At the time of their crossing of the Alps, other tribes, the Medes and Persians, settled on the Iranian plateau and conquered the land on the eastern side of the Mediterranean Sea. Further conquest was stopped by the Greeks, their rivals.

They still enjoyed yoghurt, cheese, and shish kebab in Persia, but a new substance was added to their diet—sugar. Plenty of sugar—fat was beautiful in Persia. They liked sweet and sour sauces also and large amounts of powdered walnuts or almonds to thicken sweet dishes.

Science has not found the answer to the human craving for sweet things. For centuries, honey had been the only sweetener, although sugar canes had been crushed in a primitive press in India. Sugar cane is a gigantic grass. It grows twenty-five or more feet high in a warm climate where there is plenty of rainfall. The stalks are about two inches in diameter, and like bamboo, they have segments or sections three to eight feet long. They are crushed between rollers to extract the juice which is then boiled and evaporated into a heavy syrup and crystals. The crystals are separated to become brown sugar, and the syrup molasses. Other sources are beet sugar and the maple tree, but the sugar cane is our chief supplier.

The Persians invented the very sweet pastry baklava, and they added honey or marmalade made of fruit and sugar to their yoghurt. Similarly, Americans find yoghurt more to their liking if sweetened fruit is added; plain yoghurt is a taste that needs to be acquired like buttermilk or cottage cheese.

The Caucasus Mountains between India and Central Asia are extremely high. They are safe from wind and snow only a few weeks of the year. The Aryans who crossed over the passes were very courageous. Their course was rewarded when they found fertile lands near the River Sind. These tall fair-haired conquerors remained in India to force their ways and religion on those who had settled in the Indus River Valley. In spite of rules to the contrary, they married some of the darker-skinned people living there. Their children were the ancestors of the modern Hindu race.

They called their god Brahma, and the priests who represented him were Brahmins, the highest caste. They divided the warriors into one caste, the merchants into another, and the slaves and the conquered were forced into the lowest caste. They were required to till the soil. When Buddha, a prince of India, taught kindness to all men and a reverence for all living things, a diet of meat—especially beef—was no longer permissible. The orthodox Hindu is a vegetarian. However, the Moslems, the followers of Mohammed, also invaded India, and while they prohibit pork, other meat is permissible.

A young Brahmin explains the law in a temple at Benares. From *Le Magasin Pittoresque*, Paris, 1840.   *New York Public Library, Picture Collection.*

India receives World Bank Loans for production of high-yielding foodgrain seeds. At the experimental farm of the Uttar Pradesh Agricultural University near Delhi, workers carve the soil to define the boundary between wheat and barley crops.   *United Nations.*

When the Aryans settled in India, they brought their knowledge of honey and milk products to the diet of curry and vegetables and fruits that had already been established. Wheat was grown in northern India and a way of cooking was developed that is distinctive to that region alone. Americans are not as well acquainted with it as they are with the cuisines of other countries, and they often mistake a soggy stew flavored with a blend of strange spices as curry. It is true that interesting spices are added to create a delicate or a hot flavor according to the tastes of each particular family. The spices are not added all at once, and they are generally cooked in oil or *ghee* before the meat or vegetables are cooked with them. *Ghee* is butter that has been boiled until the milky residue falls to the bottom of the pan and the oil comes to the surface. When the oil is poured off for preservation and use, it keeps much longer than ordinary butter.

The *chapati* that we learned to make in the first chapter is served daily with vegetable or meat curry, yoghurt, and fruit. Yoghurt makes a good contrast to a well-seasoned dish as does a well-cooked bland rice.

Rice was probably cultivated by the early settlers on the Indus River. It is the staple grain in southern India, growing wild all across southern Asia wherever it is extremely moist. As it needs to stand in water during most of its life, the seeds are sown in beds of liquid mud. They are transplanted when the plants are two or three inches high. Their growth is completed in standing water until the fields are drained at harvest time. In India, the seeds are separated from the stalks by the trampling hoofs of oxen. A hull remains that must be removed before the rice is eaten. It is generally removed by pounding in stone mortars in the kitchens of Indian homes.

In some areas of India, astrologers are consulted before the rice is planted. They give all the directions about sowing, even the garments that the sowers should wear. A prayer is said over the first seeds sown and a flower is placed above them. The people believe that the gods will be angered by obscene language, uncleanliness, or the eating of pork and oily fish near the rice in the fields or the threshing floor. The pounding of rice must be done far from the field so that the standing crop is not weakened. It is also believed that the wrath of the goddess Pattini shown by droughts or plagues is appeased by a coconut fight. For several days, the men of the village line up thirty yards apart tossing coconuts at nuts that have been thrown into the space between. When a nut is broken by a coconut, the performance is concluded by a feast. Priests are

66

Workers at the experimental farm of the Central Rice Research Institute in Cuttack trying out clonal propagation.   *United Nations.*

also given food offerings when the aid of the goddess is requested.

Other Indo-European tribes called Slavs dwelt in widely scattered settlements between the North Sea and the Black and Caspian seas. They were the ancestors of the Polish, the Czechoslovakian, Yugoslavian, Bulgarian, and the majority of the Russian people. They were not nomads. They were interested in growing grain. They endured long and severe winters as well as the marauding raids of nomads to grow crops. Once they quaked in fear when the Huns, a tribe of nomads under the leadership of the fierce Attila, strode across the plains. Eventually, his descendants also became grain growers in the area that is now Hungary.

Slowly the Slavs spread out in all directions, especially along the rivers of eastern Russia where they built trading settlements to sell grain and furs to the Byzantine empire. Because the Slavs were poorly organized, they invited a Viking chief named Rurik to govern them. He was the leader of a tribe called the Rus. He accepted and founded the first organized government of Russia in Kiev.

For at least two thousand years, wheat has been cultivated in the Russian Ukraine above the Black Sea and in Eastern Europe. The United States obtained seeds of the wheat from that area when we started to cultivate the productive Great Plains. The climate of both areas is similar and the yield is generally equal. In some areas of our northern plains and the plains of Russia and Eastern Europe, the winters are so severe that the ground is deeply frozen. Therefore they grow wheat which is planted only in the spring and harvested a little later than winter wheat which is planted in the fall. It remains dormant in the ground if the winter is not too severe and grows again at the first signs of spring.

Mongols rout Russians northeast of Moscow, 1238. From a 16th Century miniature.
Horizon Magazine, Winter, 1968, N.Y. *New York Public Library, Picture Collection.*

The ancient Slavs were sun worshippers. They honored their god in the spring by cooking and eating small round golden pancakes called *blini* which were made to look like the sun and are still served today. Rurik brought a tradition of rich cream sauces and a cake of apples and cherries from his Scandinavian homeland. Later the Mongols who invaded Russia brought sauerkraut and tea from the Chinese.

Easter is a very special day in Russia. The day is even observed by people who have forsaken the beliefs of the Greek Orthodox Church to adopt the rule of the Soviet Union. The return of spring was celebrated in pre-Christian days with the giving of exquisitely dyed eggs. The custom survived into the Christian era when families and friends exchanged painted eggs with the words "Christ is Risen" painted upon them. First a design was painted on the eggshell with beeswax and the egg was dipped

Street scene in old Bukhara, Uzbek, U.S.S.R. *United Nations photo by P. Teuscher.*

into dye. Each successive dyeing was preceded by an elaboration of the design in this manner. The result was an intricate and beautiful geometric pattern traced in brilliant colors.

The Easter feast begins with the serving of ham or turkey and *pashka*, made of nuts, fruit, heavy cream, and pot cheese. A special cake called *kulich* baked in a long cylindrical shape is placed on the table in the midst of candles along with the Easter eggs and the *pashka* early on the Saturday before Easter. Sometimes the *kulich* is cut in rounds and sampled before the feast by eager relatives and friends. The following recipe does not make as monumental a cake as the traditionally huge cake placed upon the Russian Easter table, but the same ingredients are used and it is just as tasty. Other traditional recipes from the lands of the steppes are included.

⚜ KULICH / A Russian Easter Cake

Ingredients	Utensils
Flour (all-purpose)	Large and small bowls
Sugar	Wooden spoon
Salt	Coffee can (1 lb or
Yeast	454 grams)
Vanilla	Aluminum foil
Milk	Sauce pan
Eggs	Towel
Butter or margarine	Measuring spoons
Cardamom	Measuring cups or metric
Golden raisins	measuring containers
Mixed candied fruits	Cooling rack
Sliced almonds	
Powdered sugar	
Lemon juice	

CAKE RECIPE

Standard	*Metric*
3 cups sifted all-purpose flour	384 grams
1/4 cup sugar	60 grams
1/4 teaspoon salt	3 grams
1 package dry yeast	7 grams
1/2 cup milk	120 ml
1/4 cup butter or margarine	60 grams
2 eggs	
1/2 teaspoon vanilla	5 ml
dash of cardamom	
1/4 cup of the following:	
Golden raisins	40 grams
Mixed candied fruit	40 grams
Sliced almonds	35 grams

ICING RECIPE

1 cup powdered sugar	140 grams
2 tablespoons milk	30 ml
1/2 teaspoon lemon juice	5 ml

METHOD

Combine 1 cup flour, sugar, salt, yeast, and cardamom in a large bowl. Heat butter, milk, and vanilla in a sauce pan until it is warm—not hot. Gradually pour liquid over dry ingredients in bowl.

With a wooden spoon, beat in eggs and remaining flour. Mix entire mixture well.

Turn dough onto a floured surface and knead five minutes. Add almonds, raisins, and mixed fruit. Knead five more minutes.

Place dough in a well-greased bowl. Cover with a towel; let rise in a warm place until it is double in size.

Grease coffee can. Punch dough down and place it in the coffee can. Wrap can in greased aluminum foil. Let foil extend two inches above the rim. Let dough rise again for one hour.

Bake in oven preheated to 350° F (177° C) for one hour. Remove and let cool on a rack.

Mix powdered sugar, milk, and lemon juice in a small bowl. Ice the top of the cake. Let a little icing run down the sides to give the appearance of a candle.

RICE AND SPICE OF INDIA / Massale Dar Pilau

Ingredients	Utensils
Long grain rice	Medium and large sauce pans
Onions	Colander
Butter	Small mortar and pestle for
Yoghurt (unflavored)	crushing spices
Salt	Measuring spoons
Garlic	Measuring cups or metric
Chicken broth	measuring containers
Turmeric	
Ginger	
Cardamom seeds	
Cayenne pepper	
Tomatoes	

RECIPE

Standard	Metric
1 cup rice	240 grams
1/2 cup chopped onions	120 grams
3 tablespoons butter	45 grams
1/2 cup unflavored yoghurt	225 grams
3/4 teaspoon salt	4 grams
1 clove garlic, finely chopped	
3 cardamom seeds, crushed in mortar and pestle	
1/4 teaspoon ground turmeric	
1/4 teaspoon ground ginger	
1/4 teaspoon cayenne pepper	
1 1/2 cups chicken broth	360 ml
3–4 tomatoes cut in wedges	

METHOD

Let rice soak for twenty minutes in medium-size sauce pan. In large sauce pan, cook onions in butter until they are brown.

Drain rice in colander. Add to onions in larger sauce pan and cook five minutes. Add spices, garlic, and yoghurt. Cook five minutes more.

Add chicken broth. Cover with lid. Bring rice and broth mixture to a boil. Reduce to simmer and cook thirty minutes with the lid on.

Serve on a plate and garnish with fresh tomato wedges.

Serves 4.

BLINI

Blini is the Russian version of the pancake served at every meal during the "butter season" before Lent. It is a small pancake—one person could eat two or three dozen topped with caviar, butter, or sour cream.

Ingredients	*Utensils*
Yeast	Flour sifter
Sugar	Rubber spatula
Milk	Wooden spoon
Flour (all-purpose)	Large and medium size
Buckwheat flour	bowls
(optional)	Sauce pan
Salt	Griddle
Eggs	Wire whisk (or electric
Butter	mixer)
Sour cream	Measuring spoons
Whipped cream	Measuring cups or metric
Caviar or salmon (optional)	measuring containers

RECITE

Standard	*Metric*
1 package dry yeast	7 grams
1/4 cup lukewarm water	60 ml
1 teaspoon sugar	5 grams
2 cups milk, scalded and	
cooled to lukewarm	480 ml
1 teaspoon salt	5 grams
2 cups all-purpose flour or	280 grams
1 cup all-purpose flour and	140 grams
1 cup buckwheat flour	140 grams
3 large eggs, separated	
1/4 lb butter or margarine	120 grams
1/2 cup whipped cream	120 ml
1/2 lb caviar or salmon	
(optional)	250 grams
1 cup sour cream	240 ml

METHOD

In a large bowl, soak yeast, warm water, and sugar. Add 1 cup flour and stir with wooden spoon. Cover and let rise for one half hour.

Add remaining flour, milk, and egg yolks. Beat well with wooden spoon until the batter is smooth. Let rise again for one hour. Add three tablespoons melted butter.

Beat egg whites with wire whisk or electric mixer until stiff enough to stand in peaks. Fold into batter. Then fold in cream that has been whipped.

Heat griddle. Add teaspoon of butter. Pour in one table-spoon pancake batter. Cook for one minute. Turn and cook 1/2 minute. Keep each pancake warm in low oven.

Serve with melted butter, sour cream, and caviar or smoked salmon broken into small pieces.

Yield: 24.

Czusztatoit Palacsinta / *Palashint-a*

Rich Dessert Pancakes of Hungary

When you try to pronounce some Hungarian words, you probably find it very difficult because the language of Hungary has no relationship to the other languages of Europe. The Huns and their cousins, the Magyars, who finally settled down on the great wheat belt that borders the river Danube are a colorful people who love music with their good food.

There is a well-known legend in Hungary that tells the story of the birth of their nation. It seems that Nimrod left the tower of Babel after the confusion of tongues and migrated to a new land in Central Asia. There he had two sons, Magyar and Hunyor. While hunting one day, the two young men followed a white stag into a delightful country. They obtained permission from their father to settle there. Each founded a great nation.

Many, many years later, the more warlike Huns left to found the brief but fearsome empire on the plains of Asia under their leader Attila. After the death of Attila, his son escaped the fury of the nations to live in a territory of the Greeks. Finally one of his grandsons, Arpad, achieved the dream of occupying the land that is present-day Hungary. During his reign, a war was being waged with a tribe occupying nearby forests and mountains until the discovery was made that the enemy was, in fact, their cousins, the Magyars. They made peace and joined in founding a new nation.

Hungary has had many conquerors since its beginnings. Budapest, its capital on the Danube, suffered much damage during World War II. Many of the exterior walls that fell during the bombing raids revealed facades built during the Middle Ages. Many of the buildings have been rebuilt to look as they did during that time. Eight of the bridges crossing the river were rebuilt, and a new one was added called the Arpad, after the nation's founder. Budapest is one of the largest centers of flour milling in Europe. It is in the center of a vast wheat area.

Hungarian food is distinctive and tasty. One of their national dishes, gulyas (goulash), is made in a stewpot similar to that used by the nomads centuries ago. Red onions are cooked in lard—never butter—until they are golden. The cubed beef is added and cooked with the onions until the broth is thickened. Next, a few teaspoons of paprika, brought by the Turks to Hungary, diced potatoes, carrots, salt, pepper, and a few caraway seeds are added. Having gulyas served over noodles made of flour, eggs and water, with a dessert of Palacsintas with a filling of apricot jam, is the tastiest dinner imaginable.

We can make the Palacsintas that are taken to school by almost every child in Hungary. They are best when served warm.

✤ PALACSINTA / Dessert Pancakes And Filling

Ingredients	Utensils
Butter	Wooden spoon
Sugar	Flour sifter
Flour (all-purpose)	Baking dish
Milk	Rotary egg beater
Eggs	Whisk
Vanilla	Pancake turner
Apricot jam or grated	Griddle
chocolate	Bowls

RECIPE

Standard	Metric
1/4 cup butter or margarine	60 grams
1/4 cup sugar	60 grams
1/4 teaspoon salt	1 1/4 grams
4 eggs, separated	
1/4 cup sifted flour	32 grams
1/2 cup milk	120 ml
1/4 teaspoon vanilla	3 ml
1/2 cup powdered sugar	
for sprinkling	70 grams
2 tablespoons slivered almonds	30 grams

MERINGUE TOPPING
3 egg whites
3 tablespoons sugar   45 grams
1 teaspoon vanilla   5 ml

METHOD
With a wooden spoon cream together the butter, sugar, and salt
in a large bowl. Add the flour and milk. Stir well. Add egg
yolks and stir. Beat egg whites with wire whisk or mixer until
stiff. Add vanilla to them. Fold into batter with whisk or rubber spatula. Preheat griddle on medium-hot heat. Grease.

Pour 1/4 cup batter onto griddle to make 6-inch fluffy pancakes. Brown lightly on one side. Remove with pancake turner
to a baking dish. Sprinkle a little powdered sugar and thinly
spread apricot jam or grated chocolate.

Continue stacking and filling pancakes in baking dish until
there are five or six layers.

Make the meringue by beating egg whites with clean, dry
whisk or mixer. Add vanilla and sugar and continue beating.
Pile the mixture on the stacked pancakes in the baking dish.
Top with slivered almonds.

Brown in slow oven (325° F or 163° C) until the meringue
is set and golden. Serve warm pie fashion.

Serves 6.

BAKLAVA

Ingredients	*Utensils*
5 sheets phyllo pastry	Loaf tin
Walnuts or almonds	Measuring cups
Brown sugar	Bowl
Butter	Sauce pan
White sugar	Wooden spoon
Lemon juice	

Standard	*Metric*
Filling:	
1 cup finely ground walnuts or almonds	150 grams
1/4 cup melted butter	52 grams
1/3 cup firmly packed brown sugar	62 grams
Syrup:	
1 cup sugar	140 grams
1/2 cup water	120 ml
2 teaspoons lemon juice	10 ml

N.B.: Phyllo pastry sheets obtainable at Middle Eastern or Greek food stores. Frozen strudel sheets may be used after thawing.

METHOD
Preheat oven to 350° F (177° C).

Cut phyllo pastry to fit the loaf tin (or fold each one in half). Place two sheets on bottom of pan that has been lightly greased with butter. Spread a layer of the filling—melted butter, brown sugar, and walnuts that have been well blended. Place two more sheets of pastry over filling. Repeat with a layer of filling—4 layers in all.

Repeat two times more and top with a layer of phyllo pastry.

In sauce pan, boil sugar, water, and lemon juice for five minutes. Pour half over pastry layers. Bake for 35 minutes.

Remove from oven. Cut baklava into diagonal sections while it is still in the pan. Cut again the other way to form diamond shapes.

Serve warm. Pour remaining syrup over each section.

Serves 6.

❧ 6 ❧
Bows and Bowls of Rice

They don't say "How are you today?" in China. They say "Have you had your rice today?" when they greet one another. The polite answer is "Yes, I have had a sufficiency, thank you." The answer is the same whether one has just finished a large bowlful or has not tasted a spoonful in days.

Rice is more than a favorite food—it is sacred to the Chinese. Millions of lives are dependent upon a successful harvest, and villages are governed by its seasons of growth, its planting and harvesting. It is used in celebrations and holidays. The custom of showering it upon the bride and groom began at Chinese wedding ceremonies. This is the way that the couple's friends wish them the blessing of many children, because rice is a symbol of fertility and of life. It is also a symbol of cleanliness. Rice straw mats have a definite place on each floor. Rice ropes are placed over doors at the New Year's festivities and small rice cakes are placed on family altars.

China is an immense country and there are regional styles of cooking that vary from one area to another, just as they do in the United States and other countries. However, no other people have developed the preparation of food into as serious an art as the Chinese. Just as a painter or a musician considers definite principles of harmony or the scientific relationship of colors on the color wheel, so does a master chef of China

Chinese Relief, Ch'ien Lung Period. Screen panel: No. 4 of eight-fold screen. Young plants fill the wide pastures: rice fields and a panorama of city and country.   *The Metropolitan Museum of Art, Kennedy Fund, 1913.*

Chinese Relief, Ch'ien Lung Period. Screen panel: No. 7 of eight-fold screen. The fragrance of the rice harvest fills the fields: cultivation, harvesting, threshing, and storing of rice. *The Metropolitan Museum of Art, Kennedy Fund, 1913.*

81

Chinese Painting,
Ming Dynasty.
Spring Festival on the River.
*The Metropolitan Museum
of Art, Fletcher Fund, 1947.*

83

work with five primary flavors and their complements. Sour, pungent, bitter, sweet, and salty must be blended harmoniously to create the best flavor. A Chinese cook also considers aroma, color, and texture. The texture of food is emphasized more than it is in Europe, and the rule of opposites is applied. As a designer opposes dark against light or rough against smooth to emphasize the center of interest in his painting, a Chinese chef contrasts crisp and crunchy food with soft and bland. For example, rice is served with crunchy, crisp vegetables. The vegetables should also be cooked without dimming their pure bright color. A great deal of time is, therefore, spent in preparing and slicing the food, but it is rapidly cooked in a little hot oil to retain its color. This style of cooking has evolved over thousands of years.

There were farmers in China when Noah built the ark in the land near the Tigris and Euphrates rivers. China was building a kingdom along the Yellow River while the pyramids were being built in Egypt. The kingdom was well over one thousand years old when the stately Parthenon first glistened under Athenian skies. No one knows where the first settlers of China came from nor when they arrived. Chinese legends tell of their leader, Fu Hi, who taught them to live in groups of families, to tame and herd sheep, to fish, and to keep fowl for food and eggs. One thousand years later, Shen Nung, another legendary leader, taught them to plow the ground with an iron plow, to plant wheat and millet seeds, and to live on fruit and the grain of the harvests. He was called "the Divine Farmer." He also taught them to refertilize the soil with any old decaying thing—even clothing—although the soil was and is unusually fertile in the north because dust rich in iron and decayed vegetable matter has been blown for centuries from the plains and mountains of Asia to rest on the Yellow River area. The dust colors the waters of the river. The fertility of the land has never diminished. When the population became dense, farmers slowly pushed their way into other parts of China. They cut away forest, drained marshes, plowed the land, and ground the grain in mills that were powered by water wheels beside rivers and streams. In 780 B.C. Emperor Huang Ti made a kingdom of all the groups that resided in China. He supervised the building of roads so that his people could travel to markets and fairs that were held in the spring when the grain was planted. He elevated cookery to an art.

Emperor Han Shu taught his subjects to grow rice. Each spring he planted three rows with great ceremony, while each of his sons planted six rows. One of the first lessons of the Chinese child is the proper method of cooking rice. He dare not present a poorly cooked bowl after receiving instructions for he would receive a thrashing. Food is too scarce to waste.

Although the wealthy Chinese eat a large variety of food, the diet of the peasant who works on the land is limited. The idea of cutting the small amount of meat obtainable and the vegetables into paper thin fragments that could be quickly cooked with pancakes of millet or wheat or a bowl of rice probably evolved in the peasant kitchen where the fuel is extremely scarce. Soybeans are simmered for milk. They also yield a cooking oil, a sauce for flavoring, and a curd that is an exceptionally high protein food that is a "boneless meat" tasting somewhat like cheese. (Soy curd may be purchased at most markets.) On such a diet the peasant and his entire family work from dawn until dusk on their small plots. They cultivate the ground by the same primitive methods that have been used for thousands of years. They stop only to prepare a midday meal of millet or rice in a wok over an improvised stove.

Chinese agriculture falls into two divisions, the wet farming of the southern rice-growing country and the dry farming of the northern wheat and millet sections. Both areas use the same type of cheap, light, easily prepared implements. Plows that are light enough to be carried home are drawn by water buffaloes or small oxen or donkeys. The fields are painstakingly prepared and weeded by hand; the seeds are sown and reaped by hand. Four crops of rice are grown in the same soil within one year. Each crop is set out by hand and skillfully transplanted into muddy waters when the plants are twelve inches high. An occasional weeding suffices until the seeds ripen.

The millet grown in the north is cooked as a cereal and frequently served instead of rice. It is also used for vinegar and wine. Sorghum or *kaoliang,* as it is called in China, has been cultivated in Manchuria since 300 A.D. It often grows to a height of twelve feet. Its stems are used for fences or the framework of walls and ceilings. Its leaves are made into mattings and wrappings, and whatever remains is used for fuel.

This densely populated country is inhabited by one-fourth of the world's people, making fertile land in great demand. Although the Chinese have been grain farmers for forty centuries, it has not been profitable for the hard-working peasants who have been forced to lease small amounts of land from rich landowners.

A drastic governmental change occurred in the early part of the twentieth century when the people lost confidence in the rule of the Emperor and chose to become a republic. In 1949 a Communist regime came to power and a new life-style began for the peasants.

Grouped together in state farms that are owned by the government or in communes that are collectively owned by peasants who pay taxes to the government, they generally live together in barracks; men and women are assigned to their jobs in the fields, kitchens, or workshops. Gradually the age-old system of farming by hand is being replaced by an effort to introduce tractors, heavy farm machinery, and chemical fertilizers. The program of farm mechanization has recently been quickened and the aim is to have it completed by 1980. All efforts are being directed toward that goal—the peasants are leveling the land, removing rocks that would impede tractors, and straightening winding irrigation canals.

The types of plows may change, the kitchens may become

Slope land being cleared and terraced for agricultural development in
Eastern Taiwan.   *United Nations.*

87

modernized, but the basic food habits of a country rarely change, nor have they in China. Sometimes the busy workers take a moment to enjoy a little snack that may be served in their villages and even in the Chinatowns of some of our larger cities. A few similar representative recipes will follow which are interesting to make.

Bows

A *bow* is a Chinese wheat bun that is filled with meat and vegetables or a sweet paste. Traditionally steamed, as are all breads in China, they may be purchased in pastry shops steamed or baked. I bought my first *bow* from a portable stand on a street corner in Berkeley, California. It was the size of a tennis ball; the dough was light and sweet, and very white because it was steamed. A baked *bow* is golden in color.

Whether made of yeast dough or from refrigerator biscuit dough, they are fine for lunch or an afternoon snack, especially if they contain a meat and vegetable filling.

To make *bows* of biscuit dough: (10 in a package)

1. Stretch each biscuit on a flat surface until it is a four-inch round. Place 1 tablespoon of filling in center (see filling recipe below).
2. Gather edges of dough around the filling.
3. Bring the dough up to the top of the ball and press edges together.
4. Place in lightly oiled cake pan about 1 inch apart. Smooth side should be on top, fastened side on the bottom.
5. Sprinkle a few sesame seeds on each bun.
6. Bake in preheated oven 375° F (187° C) for 15 minutes until golden brown.

I. INGREDIENTS

Standard	Metric
Cut up the following until they are 1/4″ cube size:	
Meat from two chicken breasts	400 grams
1/2 cup sliced mushrooms	100 grams
1/2 cup diced celery or bamboo shoots (available canned at most markets)	100 grams
1/2 cup sliced water chestnuts (also available canned)	100 grams
1 green onion stalk and bulb, finely chopped	75 grams
Place in bowl:	
1 teaspoon cornstarch	5 grams
1 teaspoon soy sauce	5 ml
1 teaspoon sugar	5 grams
1 teaspoon dry sherry	5 ml
2 tablespoons oil for frying	30 ml

METHOD

Place skillet or wok on high heat. Add 2 tablespoons of oil. Stir fry all ingredients (chicken, mushrooms, bamboo shoots, onions, and water chestnuts) until meat is cooked—about 2 minutes. Add seasoning mixed together in bowl. Stir until thick. Remove from skillet and place in bowl to use as filling for bows.

II. INGREDIENTS

Standard	Metric
1 cup ground beef	250 grams
10 water chestnuts, sliced fine	50 grams
2 whole green onions, chopped	100 grams
1 small garlic clove, crushed	50 grams

Seasoning in bowl:

1 1/2 teaspoons curry powder	10 grams
1 teaspoon salt	5 grams
2 tablespoons soy sauce	30 ml
2 tablespoons catsup	30 ml
2 tablespoons peanut oil	30 ml

METHOD

Heat skillet or wok. Add oil and garlic. Stir fry meat until it is brown. Add onions and water chestnuts—stir one minute. Add seasoning that has been combined in small bowl. Simmer one or two minutes. Set in bowl to be used as filling for bows.

Utensils that are needed for both fillings are: wok or heavy skillet, knife for chopping, measuring spoons, wooden spoon, bowls.

FLUFFY RICE CHINESE STYLE

Ingredients	*Utensils*
Rice, long grain	Heavy sauce pan with a well-fitting lid
Cold tap water	Measuring cups
	Colander

RECIPE

Standard	*Metric*
1 cup rice	240 grams
2 cups cold water	480 ml

METHOD

Place cold water in sauce pan. Add rice that has been washed under running water in a colander.

Turn heat to high and cook uncovered until the water boils. Stir once and cover with tightly fitting lid. Reduce heat to very low. Steam for 20 minutes before peeking. If rice is still a trifle hard, add two tablespoons of water and continue to steam for 10 more minutes.

Take the pot off the stove and fluff rice with forks. Serve hot.

Yield: 2 1/2 cups.

❧FRIED RICE FOR TWO

Ingredients	*Utensils*
Rice, cooked	Heavy skillet or wok
Green onions	Chopping knife
Cooked pork, chicken,	Measuring spoons
or seafood	Wooden spoon
Soy sauce	Casserole or bowl
Garlic	for serving
Egg	Measuring cups
Oil	

RECIPE

Standard	*Metric*
2 cups cooked rice	460 grams
2 green onions chopped	
(include green stems)	100 grams
1/2 lb cooked, diced pork,	
chicken, or seafood	
(about 1 cup)	226 grams
1 unbeaten egg	
1 small clove garlic, crushed	55 grams
2 tablespoons oil	30 ml
2 tablespoons soy sauce	30 ml

METHOD

Heat the skillet or wok until it is very hot. Add oil. Add garlic and brown for one minute. Add rice and cook until it is heated through (about 2 minutes). Stir constantly with wooden spoon.

Add onions, cooked meat, and soy sauce. Stir for 1 minute.

Add egg, cook and stir until egg is firm. Remove and serve hot or place in casserole to warm in oven.

Leftover rice is carefully saved in China. Enough is made to serve each person a bowl of hot steaming rice at dinner with some left over for fried rice or an afternoon snack of cold rice. Chinese children add a tablespoon of soy sauce and a tablespoon of peanut oil to one cup of cold rice for an after school treat. The Chinese prefer rice without salt, but it may be added.

Diem Sum

A tiny morsel of a delicious filling is wrapped in a four-inch-square *wun tun* wrapper or a round *suay gow pay*, steamed, and served as a tea-time snack. They were a favorite of the last empress of China, who called them *diem sums* "Little Jewels," and offered a reward of a gem to the chef who brought her a new and tasty one. They may be purchased in any Chinese pastry shop, and are frequently served in tea houses. The wrappers, made of dough, water, and eggs, are sold in supermarkets. They may be frozen for future use.

❧FILLING FOR DIEM SUM

Ingredients	Utensils
Raw chopped shrimp	Bowl
Whole green onions	Knife for chopping
Soy sauce	Measuring spoons
Egg	Measuring cup or
Wun tun or suay gow pay	metric container
wrappers	Steaming pan and rack

Standard	Metric
1/2 cup raw shrimp	125 grams
2 green onions, stems and bulbs finely chopped	75 grams
1 tablespoon soy sauce	15 ml
1 whole egg	
1/2 package wrappers	

METHOD

Mix all ingredients except wrappers in bowl to make filling. Place 1 teaspoon of filling in center of wrapper. Gather wrapper around filling. Let some of the filling be exposed at the top.

Place diem sums upright side by side on rack that is placed in pan. Place 1 1/2 cups water in bottom of pan. Cover and steam until wrappers are transparent—about 7 minutes. Serve warm.

Yield: 12.

7

Feasts, Fairs, and Frumenty

When the Celtic and Germanic tribes were pushed from the steppes into western Europe, they found a fertile but heavily forested land along the Rhine and other large rivers. There were swamps to drain and forests to clear before the grain could be cultivated, but the winters were less severe. For centuries, the people lived on a simple diet of wild fruits and nuts, milk, cheese, grain porridge, fish, wild fowl, and deer of the forest. Their homes were made of mud and wooden beams. They disliked dwellings that were attached to one another. They preferred to have some land around each house, although they were grouped together in villages. A tribal chief, whose wealth was measured by the size of his herd of cattle, was elected by a general assembly of the tribesmen.

From the earliest times, all of the Indo-European families had worshipped trees. Their temples were sanctuaries in the forest where they believed the gods lived. It was, and still is, in many parts of Europe, the custom to plant a May tree before each house, or to carry a May tree from door to door to bring home the blessing that the tree spirit could bestow. Likewise, dances were held around a fresh Maypole, or boughs were decorated with grain to ensure a good crop.

Northern Europeans believed in a Grain Mother and Maiden who corresponded to the Greek and Roman goddess, Ceres,

"Tischkarte" (menu) after Slevogt. By Oskar Bangeman. *The Metropolitan Museum of Art, Harris Brisbane Dick Fund, 1928.*

and her daughter. An image of the Mother and Maiden were often fashioned from the last sheaves of the harvest and a dance was held around the figure of the maiden at the harvest feast.

Enormous changes occurred in the lives of the land-hungry Germans when they swarmed down upon the tottering Roman empire to gain well-cultivated fields for themselves. The tribal chiefs, who as cattle rustlers had fought one another, became united under a king of the Franks named Clovis, when he was only fourteen. The Franks who lived along the Rhine were the strongest tribe and the most advanced agriculturally. Another Frankish king, Charlemagne, was the greatest king of the Middle Ages, as this period of time has been designated. He annexed most of northern Europe except the British Isles and Scandinavian peninsula. The Christian Church of Rome was the only religion of his realm. It was a strong influence upon every detail of everyday living—even the foods a person should eat.

Charlemagne traveled throughout his realm concerning himself with the welfare of his people. He issued edicts on the way meat should be smoked, on how wine, cheese, and butter should be made, and on the cultivation of grain and fruit. Wherever he went his family traveled with him—he never dined without them. Unlike some of the nobles with whom he had divided the land, he was temperate in eating and drinking. Roast beef was his favorite—he demanded it every day with some fruit, bread, and cheese.

These were the days of stone castles upon hilltops, of knights and chivalry, of nobles who lived luxuriously in their castles or fought for their king, while peasants or serfs bound to the land tilled the soil to grow a little grain for themselves and much for their masters. There was plenty of timber to keep the fires roaring in the great halls of each castle. A huge fireplace was used for warmth and for cooking. A cauldron filled with bubbling vegetable broth always hung over it. A chicken or rabbit or a pease pudding tied in a cloth cooked within it. An earthen jar of frumenty (wheat soaked in hot water until it was like jelly, then cooked slowly in milk and honey) was kept warm by the heat of the fire.

"The Harvesters" by Pieter Brueghel, the Elder. *The Metropolitan Museum of Art, Rogers Fund, 1919.*

A loud blast on a hunting horn called the family and guests to dinner at nine in the morning. Imagine facing a roasted boar or a haunch of a bear or a deer at that hour of the day! The first course was followed by roasted fowl, fish, or a peacock or swan. There were plenty of ducks, geese, or chickens, but very few vegetables were served. The food was flavored with home-grown herbs. Hunks of bread ("sops") were dipped into vege-table broth. At the end of the meal, enormous pies filled with all manner of food and sweetmeats flavored with cloves and ginger were brought to the tables with great fanfare—with trumpets and banners.

"Summer" (Aestas). Engraving by Jan Van de Velde. *The Metropolitan Museum of Art, Harris Brisbane Dick Fund, 1925.*

An oak table surrounded by benches was placed at one side of the hall. It rested upon a raised platform. A cloth that needed to be frequently changed between courses covered the table. It became dirty within a few minutes as its edges were used instead of napkins. Each person was given his own cup and he shared a piece of bread, called the trencher, with his neighbor. A trencher served as a plate, and in rare cases it was placed upon a silver plate.

An exquisite silver or gold salt celler was placed in the center of the table. The lords and ladies were placed to the right of it in order of rank, while those of inferior rank were placed at the left. Young pages served the food. As long as there was plenty of it, it did not matter if it was well cooked.

While nobles and their families feasted within the castles, the serfs labored in their master's fields three days of every week. The remainder of the time they spent on their own widely scattered plots of land. Barley was the first grain cultivated by all the Europeans. It looks like wheat, but it is starchier and lacks the gluten for making a risen loaf of bread. Another grain, rye, also grew among the wheat fields of Europe as a weed. It makes a heavy dark bread that is still eaten in Europe.

More progress was made in food cultivation during the medieval period than at any time since the farmers of Jarmo planted wheat in the hills above Mesopotamia. There were

Scythe, from a 13th Century Manuscript. Viollet-le-Duc, Eugene Emmanuel. *Dictionnaire Raisonné du mobilier francais de l'Epoque Carlovingienne a la Renaissance.* Paris: Bance, 1858–1875, six vols. *New York Public Library, Picture Collection.*

several reasons for the progress. Western Europeans were no longer subject to invasions. In fact, they invaded Britain and pushed the Slavs farther east. From the Slavic farmers, they received the idea of a new type of plow. It was called the "moldboard" plow and it cut deeply into the soil instead of just scratching the surface. It had three parts—one slashed the earth, while another cut across at grass roots level, and a third neatly turned the top soil to one side. It was heavy. As many as eight oxen were needed to pull it until a new type of harness was designed for the horse that did not choke his windpipe. This and horseshoes made him as strong as an ox for pulling heavy loads.

Another improvement in farming was the three-field rotation system that was introduced during Charlemagne's reign. One field was planted at the end of the year with wheat, another with oats, peas, beans, and barley to replenish the soil. The third was allowed to rest for a season. Larger quantities of grain were ground in the many mills that were built throughout Europe. The miller became a wealthy and powerful man. But there were still many who did not receive any benefit from the technological progress.

The peasants who worked in the fields lived in crude little houses outside the castle walls. Animals as well as people shared the earthen floors. A bakestone in the center served as a fireplace and a hole in the roof, the chimney. An iron pot and hanger, a ladle and knife, some fire tongs, and perhaps a copper kettle, were hung on a wall. The peasant's wife had to trudge up a hill to the castle mill and oven to grind and bake her grain. For this privilege it was necessary to pay a tax even though she might have an oven in her cottage. Consequently, porridge was eaten more than bread, with some fish or rabbit and a few root vegetables.

Part of a poem by William Langland, an English peasant who lived in the fourteenth century, describes the condition of the serf who did not have enough to eat, especially during a poor season. In his *Vision of Piers the Plowman,* he quotes Piers saying:

I've no penny, to buy young pullets (chickens)
Nor bacon, nor geese, only two green cheeses,
Some curds, and some cream and an oaten cake,
Two bean loaves, with bran, baking for my children,
And, I say, by my soul, I have no salt bacon,
Only onions and parsley and cabbage plants.

There was one refuge for the starving. From their ample storehouses, monasteries gave grain to the needy and bread and food to the travelers. Those who withdrew from the world to live a life of discipline and prayer were the most skillful farmers of the time. Built often in desolate places, monastery fields were fruitful and abundant as soon as the swamps were drained or the forests cleared. The monks spent their time in study, prayer, and working on manuscripts and in the fields and large kitchens behind their cloistered walls. We are indebted to them for preserving cookery, the arts, and learning. Most of them lived simply on bread and water, with a small meal toward the evening. However, some monastic orders became less strict as they grew in wealth and power. Because the clergymen failed to live up to their highest traditions, many broke away from the one Church and began to worship in the new Protestant churches.

People have always had a tendency to assert their freedom in thinking and living. The growth of towns initiated another step toward independence. Fleeing serfs were considered free if they were able to maintain themselves away from their master's land for one year. Many went to towns that began to grow near the monasteries. New villages replaced the old Roman encampments that had been built beside navigable rivers, such as Chester in England, Vienna in Austria, or Cologne in Germany. Although the residents of the new towns had small

Cistercian monks tilling the fields. Engraving. *Bettmann Archive.*

vegetable gardens in the rear of their homes, they were not
able to grow enough grain to feed themselves. Luckily, the
Slavs in the East grew more than enough and were happy to
sell it to the rest of Europe.

Today there are many villages in Europe that look as if they
were in Storybook Land. The streets and buildings appear exactly as they did hundreds of years ago. In spite of a devastating war, they have been rebuilt stone for stone as they were
in the Middle Ages, but the cobblestone streets are much
cleaner. I will never forget the sight of a small shopkeeper in
Rothenburg, Germany, scrubbing the walk in front of her door
with soap and water early one morning. A large police dog rested
on a rug placed to one side. He did not put one paw on the
newly cleaned walk.

Roads to the side of highways that teem with speeding sports cars lead through fields of grain right up to the gates of the old towns. Some are entirely surrounded by walls that have lasted through the years. Beyond the gates, the architecture may vary with the country, but all the streets are narrow, the buildings are squeezed together, the second stories protrude over the streets, and all of the windows have a profusion of flowers in boxes. As in ages past, vegetables and other produce are sold in front of the steps of the town hall or church which face the central square.

The entire wall of Rothenburg, Germany, is still standing. During the Middle Ages the town spent a great amount of money on towers and walls for its protection. The slits where the soldiers stood guard are quite evident. Ornate signs hang over the doorways of the shops on the narrow streets to reveal the type of merchandise that is sold inside. Since few could read during the Middle Ages, a design of a mortar and pestle or a horseshoe or a needle and thread served instead.

Pastries and bake shops were plentiful. An old saying is still true:

In Rothenburg on the Tauber,
The cakes and pastries are in good order.

The town mayors and court officials worked hard to maintain high standards wherever food was sold, whether at the weekly markets that were generally held at the town square, or in shops facing the streets. Flour, wine, oil, sausages, and salt pork were carefully inspected for purity, freshness, and lawful packing.

Guilds set up stringent rules regulating the prices and weights of the products as well as the standards of excellence. The guilds began as an association of town workers with similar occupations who banded together for protection. They became very powerful: They decided upon the hours of the workers, the standards for the sale of the products, and they controlled their membership. If any member was found guilty of breaking a guild rule, he was expelled and was then prohibited from working at his own trade. However, most of the merchants were honest; only a few wily salesmen successfully cheated their customers by selling bread that was less than the required 3 1/2 ounce per loaf. If a village baker was caught in the act, he was dragged through the dirtiest streets in town with the "short" loaf tied to a string and hung from his neck. He might also be placed in the stocks overnight.

At certain designated times of the year, fairs were held where products from other countries as well as food were sold. All kinds of merchandise could be purchased, including jewelry, silks and satins, pots and pans, and domesticated animals, to name a few. A shopping district in London, England, is still called Mayfair, although many a May has passed since shepherds brought their sheep to sell there.

A fair is still held every year during the week before Christmas in Nürnberg, Germany. Booths covered with red and white canopies are set up in the town square facing the church with the glockenspiel (clock tower). Small wooden figures and the most delightful Christmas tree ornaments are on display (Nürnberg was known for the toys that were manufactured there), as well as gingerbread houses as only the Germans can bake and decorate, and small figures made of walnuts, prunes, and raisins. Although the city suffered damage during the bombings of World War II, it has been rebuilt and looks exactly as it appeared in the fifteenth century prints of Albrecht Dürer, one of the town's famous residents.

The agricultural development that brought better food to more people resulted in a population growth in spite of an occasional crop failure, famine, or pestilence. People became adventurous when they enjoyed a healthier diet—they embarked on nine Crusades to the distant city of Jerusalem. Although they failed to complete their objective of freeing the Holy Land from the Arabs, they brought a knowledge of other lands

Gingerbread House.   *German Information Center.*

and a taste for foods of the Near East back to Europe. Cooking techniques improved as each area introduced new spices and fruits to their cuisine. At the same time they became aware of their own distinctive traditional ways of preparing food.

✣FRUMENTY

A favorite dish during the Middle Ages often served with venison.

Ingredients	Utensils
Cracked wheat (available at supermarkets)	Measuring cups and spoons
	Medium-sized sauce pan
Milk	Colander
Cinnamon and nutmeg	
Egg yolks	
Sugar or honey	

RECIPE

Standard	Metric
1 cup cracked wheat	240 grams
4 cups water	960 ml
2 cups milk	480 ml
1/4 cup sugar or honey	60 grams
1 stick cinnamon or 1 teaspoon ground cinnamon	5 grams
1 teaspoon nutmeg	5 grams
2 egg yolks	

METHOD

Bring water to a boil in sauce pan. Add cracked wheat and reduce to low heat. Let it simmer, uncovered on low heat, for 20 minutes.

Drain the wheat. Return wheat to sauce pan. Add milk and

simmer, stirring frequently, for 15 minutes. Add sugar, cinnamon and nutmeg, and egg yolks. Cook on low heat for 10 more minutes. Stir frequently. Serve warm in bowls.

Serves 4.

✣NÜRNBERGERS / Honey Spice Cookies

Ingredients	Utensils
Egg	Rotary egg beater
Honey	Large bowl
Brown sugar	Measuring spoons and cups
Flour	Wooden spoon
Baking powder	Spatula
Orange juice	Flour sifter
Spices (cinnamon, nutmeg)	Two 9-inch-square pans or
Candied citrus peel	2 cookie sheets
Chopped almonds	Cookie cutter or
Vanilla	sharp knife
Powdered sugar	

RECIPE

Standard	Metric
1 egg	
1/2 cup honey	120 ml
1/2 cup brown sugar	120 grams
1 2/3 cups all-purpose flour	200 grams
1 teaspoon vanilla	5 ml
1 teaspoon orange rind	5 grams
1 teaspoon baking powder	5 grams
2 tablespoons orange juice	30 ml
1/3 cup chopped almonds	60 grams
1/3 cup candied citrus peel	75 grams
1 tablespoon spices	15 grams

ICING

1/2 cup powdered sugar	70 grams
2 teaspoons water	20 ml

METHOD

In a large bowl, beat the egg until light and frothy. Gradually add sugar and honey. Beat after each addition. Stir in vanilla.

Sift spices, flour, and baking powder into the egg and sugar mixture. (Sift flour before measuring.) Add citrus and almonds and stir. Add orange juice. Cover. Place in refrigerator overnight.

Next day: Either roll out the dough until it is less than 1/4 inch thick, cut into rounds with round cookie cutter, and place on greased cookie sheet, or spread dough about 1/2 inch thick into square 9-inch pan.

Bake in preheated oven 400° F (205° C) 12–15 minutes. Remove from cookie sheet with spatula or cut into 2-inch squares if in cake pan, with knife.

Cool on cooling rack and immediately glaze with icing of powdered sugar and just enough water to make it spread. It should not be runny.

Yield: 3 dozen.

STOLLEN / German Christmas Bread

Ingredients	Utensils
All-purpose flour	Sauce pan
Sugar	Large mixing bowl
Salt	Wooden spoon
Yeast	Measuring containers and
Milk	spoons
Raisins	Cookie sheet
Grated lemon peel	
Mixed candied fruit peel	
Walnuts	
Butter	
Eggs	
Candied red cherries	
Nutmeg	

RECIPE

Standard	Metric
1/2 cup milk	120 ml
1/3 cup granulated sugar	80 grams
1 package dry yeast	7 grams
4 1/4 cups all-purpose flour	595 grams
1/4 cup warm water	62 ml
2 eggs	
1/4 cup butter	10 grams
1/4 cup vegetable shortening	10 grams
1 cup raisins	200 grams
2 oz lemon peel	60 grams
8 oz candied peel	300 grams
1/2 cup candied red cherries, chopped	150 grams
1/2 cup walnuts	150 grams
1/2 teaspoon nutmeg	3 grams
1/2 teaspoon salt	3 grams

METHOD

Heat milk in sauce pan. Add sugar and salt. Stir until dissolved. Let cool. Sprinkle yeast over warm water placed in large bowl. Stir in milk mixture. Add 1 1/2 cups flour. Beat with wooden spoon until smooth. Cover and let rise in warm place for 1 1/2 hours. Add remaining flour, butter (softened), eggs, nutmeg, and candied fruits and walnuts. Knead for 5–10 minutes until fruits and nuts are well blended within the dough.

Shape into loaf. Place on greased cookie sheet. Cover with damp towel. Let rise until double in bulk, about 2 hours.

Preheat oven 375° F (191° C). Bake 30 minutes. Cool. Brush top with melted butter. Sprinkle with powdered sugar and serve.

Yield: 1 loaf.

❧ SPAETZLE / A German Noodle

Ingredients
Flour, all-purpose
Salt
Egg
Water

Utensils
Bowl
Flour sifter
Egg beater
Large sauce pan
Colander
Wooden spoon
Perforated spoon

RECIPE

Standard
2 1/3 cups flour
1 teaspoon salt
1 egg, well beaten
1/2–3/4 cup water

Metric
300 grams
5 grams

120–180 ml

METHOD

Sift flour and salt into bowl. Add well-beaten egg and mix. Add water gradually—batter should be stiff but smooth. Fill sauce pan 3/4 full with water. Bring to boil. Add 1/2 teaspoon salt.

Place colander above sauce pan. Do not let it touch boiling water. Put some of the dough in colander. Force it through holes with wooden spoon. Cook spaetzle in boiling water 5–8 minutes. Remove from water with perforated spoon. Repeat until all of the dough is used.

Serve in side dish with meat or fowl. Sprinkle caraway seeds or Parmesan cheese or dots of butter over hot spaetzle.

Yield: 4 servings.

❧8❧
Pancakes and Oatmeal

"But hark, I hear the pancake bell,
and fritters make a gallant smell."

Poor Robin's Almanack 1964

Over 500 years ago the bell rang in the parish church of Saint Peter and Saint Paul in the little village of Olney, England. The bell was a signal for all in the village to come to the church for confession. It was Shrove Tuesday. The next day, Ash Wednesday, was the beginning of the forty days of Lent decreed by the Church as a time of fasting in all of Europe. When a person concluded his confession, he was given a small cake, a "shriving cake," to indicate that he had been "shriven" of his sins. Housewives usually spent the remainder of the day baking pancakes to use up the fats that were forbidden during Lent. The ingredients of the pancakes were symbolic of wholesome qualities: flour, the staff of life, eggs for creation, milk for purity.

One housewife, on this particular day, started her baking before confession, and she became so engrossed in her task that she forgot the time. The bell caught her unawares, but off she went, griddle in hand, apron on, to the church. She started a tradition in Olney. Every year thereafter the housewives of Olney have run a race of 415 yards from the village well to the

The Pancake Race in Olney, England, as contrasted with the race in Liberal, Kansas, each Shrove Tuesday. *Chamber of Commerce, Liberal, Kansas.*

112

church steps. They are required to wear a scarf on their heads, an apron, and to carry a griddle with a pancake therein. The pancake must be flipped three times, once at the beginning, once in the middle, and once at the end of the race. If they drop their pancake, they are not disqualified, but they must take the time to retrieve it in order to end the race with the pancake in the skillet. The winner receives a prayer book and a "Kiss of Peace" from the bell ringer. The church bells ring every year at 11:15 A.M. on Shrove Tuesday. After the Reformation, when the Protestant Church of England became the church of the realm, they were called "the Pancake Bells."

Some people in Liberal, Kansas, saw a picture of the race in Olney. In 1950, they made arrangements with the Vicar of the Church of St. Peter and St. Paul to enter the competition. A 415-yard course was laid out in Liberal. Because of the difference in time, the race actually begins a little later than the one in England, but as soon as a winner is proclaimed in Liberal, the time is compared with that of the competitor across the sea by transatlantic telephone. The winning town receives the trophy: a silver pancake griddle with the names of the past winners engraved upon it.

In other parts of England children go about the villages asking for a treat for Shrovetide much as American boys and girls in the United States do on Halloween. They sing songs to warn the householder of their coming.

> *Give me some pancakes and then I'll be gone*
> *But if you give me none*
> *I'll throw a great stone,*
> *And down your house will come.*

Throughout England, the ringing of the pancake bell in local churches has been a signal for school children, apprentices, and working men to leave their chores for a day of sports, such as egg rolling, rope pulling, and football, and, of course, a pan-

Preparing to ring the Pancake Bell at St. Mary's, Mortlake, West London. *Sphere* Magazine, London. *New York Public Library, Picture Collection.*

cake feast with cakes made by recipes that have been cherished for generations. For many years a rugged match of football has been played each Shrove Tuesday in the town of Ashbourne, England. It begins at 2:00 P.M., when a multicolored ball is tossed in the town center. The receiving team tries to get it to the edge of the other side of town either by street or by stream. In another community the married men play against a team of single men in a similar game of football. At the end of the game, the tired players are served plate-sized pancakes, as many as they can eat.

The residents of Apsley Old Hall in Nottinghamshire have invited the neighboring poor families to their mansion every Shrove Tuesday. They provide the skillets and the butter, and each mother makes the pancakes for her family. When a pancake

Shrove Tuesday from *Graphic* Magazine, London, 1870. *New York Public Library, Picture Collection.*

needs turning, she must toss it and catch it with the uncooked side downward. Many are the mishaps and many the roars of laughter.

Another interesting ceremony of Tossing the Pancake takes

place each year in Westminster School in London, England. According to tradition, the school cook enters the great hall attired in his tall white hat, apron, and white jacket, carrying a skillet with a pancake. He is followed by the dean and the headmaster of the school. The students, all boys, have assembled and are seated facing a high bar that runs across the center of the hall. Upper school boys are on one side of the bar, those of the lower school (grade) are on the other side. Under the bar, representatives from each grade stand in readiness. At a signal given by the headmaster, the cook tosses the pancake over the bar. The contestants dive ferociously for the pancake. After two minutes of violent tussling, the headmaster calls time. The boy with the largest piece of pancake in his hand is the winner. He receives a monetary award, and so does the cook for successfully throwing the pancake over the bar.

From the shores of the English Channel to the steppes of Russia, Shrove Tuesday is a day of merriment. Parades, balls, costume parties, and the traditional feast of pancakes are the order of the day. Children in Luxembourg receive gifts of waffles and pancakes on *Fatten Donneschdeg* after singing a song that promises good health to the donors and bad luck to the stingy. Belgian boys and girls celebrate with a picnic of apples, bacon bits, and *koebakken* (pancakes). The Irish find charms in their pancakes that foretell the future, and Hungarian children flip their own pancakes while holding a coin in their left hand for good luck. There are carnivals and fairs and tiny *blini* in Russia. Germans prefer *fastnacht kuckens,* a type of doughnut, while the French crepes are folded to swim in liqueurs.

Long before the pancake bell first rang in England, the Angles, Saxons, and Jutes, who came from Germany when the Roman legions left the islands, found oats growing wild within Stonehenge on Salisbury Plain. This mysterious arrangement of gigantic stones was thought to have been constructed by the Celts who preceded them. However, it has been discovered that waves of

116

farmers crossed the Mediterranean and arrived in Britain around 3000 B.C. They grew wheat. Stonehenge, it is now believed, was built as a gigantic calendar to reveal the movements of the sun, stars, and moon by shadows cast by the huge stones. The priests who studied the shadows told the people the best time to plant their crops. Hundreds of similar monuments have been found throughout Britain and in Brittany, across the channel, although they are not as elaborate as Stonehenge.

The climate was warmer and sunnier in those days. The island was fertile and every kind of grain could be grown to produce two harvests a year. It is a cold and misty land now, although still fertile, but colder in the north. It lends itself especially well to the cultivation of oats, the grain that leads all others in food value. Oats belong to the same family as wheat and the other grains. It may have developed from wild grass. It grows to a height of two to four feet on very slender stalks. Tiny branches end with a seed that is covered by a protective husk. Seeds may be scattered over a plowed field or planted in rows in the spring.

Oatmeal, a favorite of the Irish and Scots, is rich in protein. Scottish or Irish oatmeal may be purchased in specialty stores. It looks a little like cracked wheat. The grains have been simply cut with a stone. American brands of rolled oats require less cooking as they have been precooked and steamed on rotating broilers.

Years ago, agriculture was the principal occupation of the British people. They depended upon their own crops of wheat, barley, and oats, and ground their grain in local mills. Their plows were made in the local smithy. They sold the surplus to the towns where they bought some luxuries and necessities.

However, the Industrial Revolution brought far-reaching changes because industry became more important than agriculture. Manufacturers wanted to be free to import as well as export produce. Therefore, the old Corn Laws (all grains are called "corn" in Britain) which had protected the farmer from

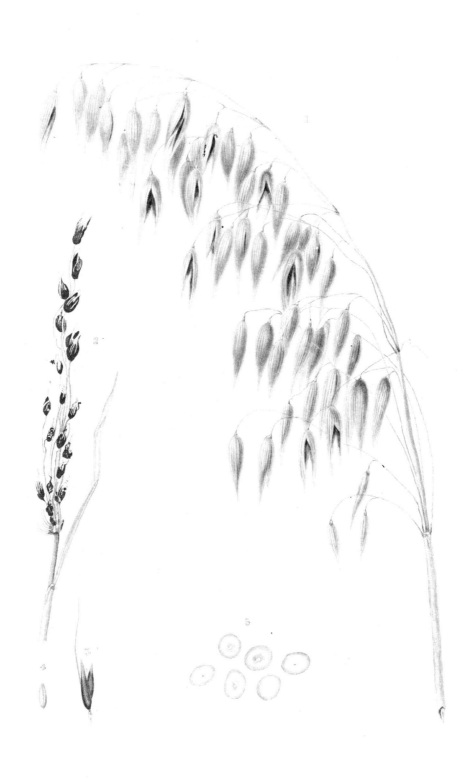

competition with suppliers of grain from other countries were repealed.

Today, only one person in six earns a living by farming in England. More grain is imported from other countries than in the past, although wheat, barley, and oats are still the principal crops.

Griddle Scones / *A Scots Pancake*

Many years ago Scotland was an independent country and its capital was Scone, which is north of Edinburgh, the present capital. There was an abbey near Scone that housed a cherished stone. It was called the Stone of Scone, or Stone of Destiny, and all Scottish rulers were crowned upon it until the year 1300, when Edward I, King of England, seized it in one of the skirmishes between England and Scotland.

Edward requested that a special throne be built with a shelf beneath the seat. The Stone of Scone was placed upon the shelf. The throne was placed in Westminster Abbey in London and has remained there to this day. It is the coronation throne for the Kings and Queens of Britain. On it they are crowned in an official ceremony.

The scones that are eaten at teatime are named for the Stone of Scone, but, hopefully, bear no resemblance to their namesake. They are light and fluffy, if a bit crusty on the outside. They are like a thick pancake.

Scone rhymes with gone, not stone.

Oats. From *New York State. Natural History Survey. Natural History of New York. N.Y. and Albany; State of N.Y. 1842–79. New York Public Library, Picture Collection.*

119

GRIDDLE SCONES

Ingredients	Utensils
Flour	Flour sifter
Baking powder	Measuring cups and spoons
Baking soda	Wooden spoon
Salt	Knife
Buttermilk	Griddle
Butter for griddle	Pancake turner
Jam or marmalade	Bowl

RECIPE

Standard	Metric
2 cups plus 2 tablespoons flour	255 grams
2 teaspoons baking powder	10 grams
1/4 teaspoon baking soda	2 grams
1/4 teaspoon salt	2 grams
3/4 cup buttermilk	180 ml

METHOD

Sift flour, baking powder, soda, and salt into a large bowl. Add the buttermilk all at once and stir with a wooden spoon. Turn the dough out on a floured board and separate into two portions. Pat each portion into the size of a dessert plate or 6–8 inches in diameter. Cut each circle into four pie-shaped wedges. Bake on a medium-hot, greased griddle for 10 minutes. Turn on the other side with a pancake turner, and bake for 10 more minutes.

Serve warm with butter, jam, or marmalade.

Serves 4–6.

Shrovetide Pancakes

Streams of children call in groups from nine in the morning until three in the afternoon at the homes of village housewives in England on Shrove Tuesday preceding Lent.

They politely say "Please a pancake," or sing an appropriate song. At some homes they get just what they ask for. In others they may get a bit of candy or an orange. They must walk to gather their treats. In some places the journeys end with a pancake-eating contest.

❧SHROVETIDE PANCAKES

Ingredients	Utensils
Flour	Bowl
Milk	Wire whisk
Eggs	Pancake turner
Salt	Griddle

RECIPE

Standard	Metric
2 eggs	
1 1/4 cups flour	177 grams
2 cups milk	480 ml
1/4 teaspoon salt	2 grams

METHOD

Measure flour and salt into a bowl and make a well in the middle. Break the eggs into the well and pour a little of the milk into it. With a wire whisk, beat the eggs and milk slowly, adding a little of the surrounding flour. Add the milk as you beat. When all the flour and milk are in, beat the whole until all the lumps are gone.

Grease the skillet. Pour a teacup of batter onto the hot skillet and bake until the surface is bubbly. Turn with pancake turner and bake on other side for a minute. Pancakes should be the size of a dinner plate. Serve hot.

Serves 4.

Guy Fawkes Cake

"Please to remember the fifth of November
Gunpowder, Treason, and Plot."

November fifth is a day of fun for boys and girls in England. It seems that a certain Guy Fawkes tried to blow up the Houses of Parliament on November 5, 1605, but he failed miserably. He was caught in the act and hung for the unsuccessful attempt.

Now he is hung in effigy—or make believe—and the day is celebrated with a cake that is frosted to look like an explosion or is made in the shape of a man. The cake is accompanied with a gala display of fireworks similar to the American Fourth of July.

⚜GUY FAWKES CAKE

Ingredients	*Utensils*
Flour	Flour sifter
Baking powder	Measuring spoons and cups
Sugar	Bowls
Eggs	Rotary eggbeater
Strawberry jam	Two square cake pans
Salt	Wax paper
Powdered sugar	Cooling rack
Lemon juice	Rubber spatula
Red food coloring	

RECIPE

Standard	Metric
3 eggs	
1 cup cake flour	120 grams
1 teaspoon baking powder	5 grams
1/4 cup sugar	60 grams
3 tablespoons strawberry jam	45 ml
1 tablespoon boiling water	15 ml
Pinch of salt	
1 lb package powdered sugar	500 grams
3 tablespoons lemon juice	45 ml
Few drops red food coloring	

METHOD

Sift together the flour, baking powder, and salt into a large bowl. Place eggs and sugar in another bowl. Beat eggs and sugar with a rotary egg beater until they are thick and frothy. Add one tablespoon of boiling water into the eggs and sugar, and quickly fold the flour mixture into the egg mixture with rubber spatula. Spread the batter into two greased and paper-lined cake pans. Bake in hot oven, 450° F (232° C) for 15 minutes. Cool on rack. Coat one cake with jam. Place one cake on top of the other.

In another bowl mix the powdered sugar and lemon juice. Frost the two-layered cake but save some of the frosting for decoration. Add food coloring to remaining frosting. With a cake decorator or wax paper folded to make a point, write the words *Guy Fawkes* and surround with zig-zag lines to resemble an explosion.

BOXTY-ON-THE-PAN

Ingredients	Utensils
Potato	Food grater
Flour (all-purpose sifted)	Griddle
Eggs	Pancake turner
Baking powder	Flour sifter
Salt	Wooden spoon
Milk	Measuring spoons
Butter	Measuring cups
Pepper	Bowl

RECIPE

Standard	Metric
1 cup cooked mashed potato	250 ml
1 cup raw potato, grated	250 ml
1 cup flour	128 grams
3 eggs	
2 teaspoons baking powder	10 grams
1/2 cup milk	120 ml
1 tablespoon melted butter	15 grams
1 teaspoon salt	5 grams
1 teaspoon pepper	5 grams

METHOD

With a food grater, grate a raw potato into a bowl. Add 1 cup cooked mashed potato. Add eggs, sifted flour, baking powder, salt, and pepper. Stir in milk and melted butter. Drop by large spoonfuls onto a hot griddle that has been greased with small amount of butter. Bake 4 minutes on each side on medium heat.

Yield: 4–6.

❧9❧
Pasta and Polenta

Wheat for pasta, corn for polenta, rice for risotto. Italy has them all, as well as luscious fruits and vegetables, and groves of olive trees for oil. No wonder the Italians like to cook and eat—and we like what they cook! It is the kind of cuisine that has a directness and clarity of flavor. You know what you are eating, and the product is excellent. It does not take years and years of study as in the case of Chinese or French cooking, nor does it have the finesse of the latter types, but it is home cooking and good cooking.

As in every country, there are regional differences in taste due to the geography and history of each section. There is more fertile soil in northern Italy. It was influenced by the early Etruscans. The south is barren, and the cooking is a result of Greek and Arab invasions. The Italian cooking that we have become most familiar with stems from the southern city of Naples. However, there are certain basic dishes that are served in every area of Italy.

One is pasta, made of flour, a little olive oil, and water, and an egg if one lives in northern Italy. Pasta has been enjoyed for years in Italian homes. Etruscan tombs reveal that these early settlers made it, although it has been mistakenly reported that Marco Polo brought the idea of noodles and spaghetti from China. He did bring ginger back to his home in Venice, a

great deal of information about the Orient, and a new way of getting there. But Italian recipes, circulated long before his return, contained recipes and directions on making several kinds of pasta. The ingredients are always the same—it is the way that the pasta is cut and served that makes the difference in name.

The Renaissance, a massive rebirth in interest in all the arts, knowledge, and science, began in Florence in the fifteenth century. Famous men of the arts, Dante and Donatello, lived there. The genius of some of the Florentine artists, Giotto, Michelangelo, Leonardo da Vinci, to name but a few, has never been surpassed. Here, cooking became a fine and respected art once again. It had been extremely simple during the Middle Ages. Only the monks retained any knowledge of classical cooking. Bread was not made again until the late Middle Ages. But the first cooking academy in Europe, called the Company of the Cauldron, was but one of the avenues through which that art was once again respected and studied. All of the twelve members of the Academy were artists who were required to create a new dish for each meeting.

Generally, Florentines had two meals a day. Platina, the author of the first printed cookbook, 1475, advocated beginning each meal with fruit. Sugar, introduced during the Crusades, had given the people a sweet tooth. Those who could afford sugar that was sold by Venetian merchants even put it in their macaroni. They also do amazing things to spinach. A dish ending in "à la Florentine or Fiorentina" is generally served with some spinach, but don't shun it for that reason, you will be pleasantly surprised.

Especially fine durum wheat grows in northern Italy where everything that is farmed is seemingly unsurpassed anywhere else in the world. Wheat is the main crop, and excellent corn,

House built for farmers under land reform program near village of Ceri, in the Maremma region near Rome. *United Nations.*

rice, and vegetables are cultivated by especially talented "green thumbs." The wheat is milled into a flour called "soglia" that holds together well when the pasta is cooked. The people in Bologna scorn machinery when they make pasta. They knead and knead the dough, and they roll it out into transparent sheets. One of their specialties, *lasagna,* is made with a superb meat sauce. Bologna is famous for its sausage, that is not to be confused with the poor substitute, bologna.

After the Italians received rice from the Arabs, they concentrated on its growth in the Po River valley. Consequently, Italian rice is among the best. They prohibited the export of its seeds, but our own Thomas Jefferson, who was extremely interested in foods, smuggled some out to see if it would grow well in the United States. It did.

Venice was always a little apart from the rest of Italy. It was founded by people who were fleeing the Huns. It began as a fishing village among its small islands. Later it traded in salt, then sugar and spice. An independent republic, its citizens became enormously wealthy when they controlled the trade in the Mediterranean after the fall of Constantinople. They were exposed to a greater variety of foods than the rest of Italy. They naturally used a great amount of fish in their cooking, but less garlic and tomato sauce. Especially fine peas are cultivated on one of the Venetian islands.

Now Venice is a fascinating place for tourists. Its streets are canals whose waves gently lap under the doors of the beautifully designed buildings that face them. Unfortunately, the first floors of many are uninhabitable as the buildings, built on piles set deeply in the mud, slowly sink. Glass blowing was developed into a fine art—Venetians introduced glassware and forks at their banquets. Exquisite examples of Vene-

Farmers working a field in the countryside near Taranto. The region has been irrigated by an aqueduct which diverts water from the Tara River.

United Nations.

Neapolitan Pizza.   *Italian Government Travel Office.*

tian glass may be purchased in shops that line the Piazza San Marco, as well as coffee from the outdoor cafes. Coffee was introduced into Europe because of Venice's trade in the Mediterranean.

Naples, south of Rome, is the home of the pizza. Many varieties are made there. They are usually pie-sized (pizza means pie). Made of leavened wheat dough, they should be eaten hot, right out of the oven. A historic food, they were enjoyed by the citizens of the unfortunate Pompcii, not far from Naples. Wealthy bakers lived there. They had their baked goods ready for sale when the lethal heat and lava descended from Mt. Vesuvius.

However, the Pompeians did not put tomato sauce on their pizzas because they had never seen a tomato. Much, much later the tomato plant, a weed growing in the corn fields of Central America, came with the corn that Spanish explorers brought back to Europe. Columbus had eaten corn in Cuba. He thought it was quite tasty. Europeans were not eager to cultivate it. The Italians were the first. They ground it into a flour and used it in a porridge called *polenta*, which replaced the old Roman *pulmentum*. It is as popular a dish in northern Italy as pasta. It is served with many sauces, or eaten as a cornmeal bread. Generally made in an unlined copper pot, it is always stirred in a clockwise direction.

We should not leave the Italian peninsula without a word about Sicily and Sardinia, the islands at the foot of Italy. Once a Greek settlement, Sicily always had a surplus of wheat. It was a granary for the Roman empire. Later Arabs conquered it and brought citrus fruit, its second crop of importance. Tomatoes, beans, figs, and a kind of grape for raisins are cultivated. Unlike Sardinia, where meat is plentiful because most of the people are sheep or goat herders, there is little meat in the Sicilian diet. The people eat a large amount of pasta and homemade bread. They make it as the ancient Greeks taught their ancestors — in a variety of sizes and shapes. In Sardinia, the bread is very flat and thin. Stacks of it are carried into the fields by herdsmen.

Sicilians are most famous for their cakes and pastries with rich fillings that are made for Christmas, Easter, weddings, or the many festivals that the people enjoy. There is at least one for every month of the year. Two of the feast days are held in honor of two beautiful young Christian maidens. Both suffered a cruel revenge by their heathen suitors when they refused to yield to them. The Feast of Saint Agatha is held each February 6 in Catania, Sicily. Traditionally, pumpkin seeds, sunflower seeds, roasted chestnuts, and strings of almond cookies are sold from carts that line the streets of Catania.

On December 13, the Feast of Saint Lucy is held in Sicily and throughout Italy. According to legend, Saint Lucy went blind

Southern Italy: special bread for wedding celebration. *Italian Government Travel Office.*

on December 13 as a result of a cruel torture. Once during a famine, while the people of the city of Syracuse, her home, were praying to her for assistance, a ship carrying grain for them was sighted at the harbor. Now, *cuccia*, made of dried chick peas and wheat kernels, is the only food served on Saint Lucy's day to express gratitude for her miraculous aid.

Luckily, *cannoli à la Siciliana*, one of the most delicious treats of Sicily and a dessert to be enjoyed in any part of the world, is not reserved for any one day of the year. The pastry was once wrapped around a piece of bamboo cane, but aluminum piping is available in most cookware shops. As the recipe on page 139 for cannoli indicates, an old broom handle cut into four-inch sections will serve very well.

This recipe is enough for two persons. It is easier to work with small amounts the first time.

Ingredients	Utensils
Flour	Flour sifter
Eggs	Fork
Oil	Baggie or saran wrap
Salt	Rolling pin
	Knife
	Large sauce pan

RECIPE

Standard	Metric
1 3/4 cups flour	248 grams
2 eggs	
2 teaspoons oil	10 ml
1/4 teaspoon salt	2 grams

METHOD

Sift the flour onto the counter. Make a well in the center of the flour. Add eggs, salt, and oil. Beat the eggs and liquid with a fork. Let a little flour come into the mixture gradually. Beat until all the flour and eggs are well mixed. Knead on a floured counter for ten minutes. Place in a baggie or cover with saran wrap. Let the dough rest one hour. It may be refrigerated until further use.

Place dough on floured counter. Gently roll it out until it is very thin. Always start from center and work out. When you have a circle about six inches in diameter, turn over and continue rolling. Press *gently* with rolling pin.

When pasta is very thin, roll it up as if you were rolling paper. With a knife cut the roll into desired thickness: for lasagna, 1 1/2 inch strips; for *fettuccine* (Italian word for noodles), 1/8 inch strips.

Unroll strips and boil in 4 cups boiling water for five minutes. Save for lasagna or serve immediately with butter and Parmesan cheese.

Uncooked pasta will keep a few weeks without refrigeration if dry and uncovered in a cool cupboard.

POLENTA

Ingredients	Utensils
Yellow cornmeal	Wooden spoon and board
Salt	Measuring cups and spoons
Hot and cold water	Sauce pan (if you wish to be authentic and have an unlined copper pot, use it)

RECIPE

Standard	Metric
1 cup yellow cornmeal	150 grams
2 cups cold water	480 ml
3 cups hot water from faucet	720 ml
1 1/2 teaspoons salt	7 grams

METHOD

Place cold water in sauce pan. Stir the cornmeal into the cold water with a wooden spoon. When there are no lumps, add hot water and salt. Place the sauce pan on low heat and simmer the polenta for an hour, stirring in a clockwise direction from time to time with a wooden spoon.

When the polenta comes easily from the side of the pan, it is cooked enough. Pour it on a wooden board and spread to the thickness of 1/2 inch. Let it cool. In Italy it is cut with a string, and served with Sauce Bolognese (recipe follows), or with milk and honey, or Parmesan cheese.

Serves 6.

SAUCE BOLOGNESE
For noodles, spaghetti, polenta, or lasagna

Ingredients	Utensils
Tomato sauce	Measuring cup and spoons
Tomato paste	Knife
Onion	Skillets (2)
Celery	Wooden spoon
Carrot	
Parsley	
Garlic	
Olive or vegetable oil	
Sugar and spices	
(nutmeg, salt, pepper,	
marjoram, bay leaf)	
Dried or fresh mushrooms	
Milk	
Water	
Ground beef and bacon	

RECIPE

Standard	Metric
Chop finely:	
1 onion	125 grams
1 stalk celery	75 grams
1 carrot	75 grams
1 small clove garlic	25 grams
1 teaspoon parsley	10 grams
4 slices cooked bacon	125 grams
1/2 cup mushrooms	125 grams
Pinch of the following:	2 grams
nutmeg, salt, pepper,	
marjoram, one bay leaf,	
whole	
1 teaspoon sugar	5 grams
1/2 cup milk	120 ml
1 (8 oz) can tomato sauce	226 ml
plus 1 (8 oz) can water	
1 (6 oz) can tomato paste	170 ml
plus 1 (6 oz) can water	
1/2 lb ground beef	250 grams

METHOD

Sauté onion in a small amount of oil in skillet until it is transparent but not brown. Add vegetables that have been chopped and cook until they are soft.

In another skillet cook the bacon, remove, and chop. Leave a small amount of bacon fat in skillet for browning the meat. Cook the meat until the reddish color has disappeared, then add mushrooms and milk, and simmer until the milk has evaporated, stirring from time to time with a wooden spoon. Add parsley, sugar, salt, pepper, nutmeg, garlic, bay leaf, and marjoram to meat. Add the sautéed vegetables in the other skillet. Add tomato sauce and water, tomato paste and water. Bring the entire mixture to a boil. Reduce heat and simmer on low heat in the uncovered skillet for at least one hour. Serve with pasta or polenta.

Serves 4, or makes 4–5 cups.

RISI E BISI

Originally served on April 25 to celebrate the Feast of Saint Mark, the patron saint of Venice. In Italy it is made using peas that are young, sweet, and tender and rice from the Po Valley.

*Ingredients for an American
version*
Onion
Butter
Olive oil
Frozen peas
Rice
Chicken broth
Ham slices or bacon
Celery
Parmesan cheese

Utensils
Large skillet
Measuring cups and spoons
Lid for skillet
Wooden spoon

RECIPE

Standard	Metric
1 onion chopped	125 grams
3 tablespoons butter	45 grams
1 tablespoon olive oil	15 ml
1/2 cup chopped celery or	125 grams
1 tablespoon celery salt	15 grams
1 teaspoon salt	5 grams
10 oz package of frozen	
peas, thawed	283 grams
1 cup uncooked rice	240 grams
3 cups chicken broth	720 ml
1/2 cup chopped ham or 4	
slices bacon	125 grams
1/3 cup Parmesan cheese	50 grams

METHOD

Sauté the chopped onion in skillet with oil and butter until the onion is transparent but not brown. Fry bacon and crumble into small pieces or fry chopped ham. Drain bacon grease. Add celery or celery salt. Add peas. Cook for two more minutes. Add rice and stir with wooden spoon. Add chicken broth and bring to a boil. Reduce to low heat. Cover skillet and simmer slowly for 25 minutes.

Add Parmesan cheese and serve in a vegetable dish or large bowl.

Serves 6–8.

❧COOL RISE PIZZA

Ingredients	*Utensils*
Yeast	Measuring cups and spoons
Salt	Bowl
Flour, all-purpose	Wooden spoon
Oil	Saran wrap and wax paper
Water	Rolling pin
Italian tomato sauce	2 small pizza pans
Oregano	
Parmesan cheese	
Mozzarella cheese	

RECIPE

Standard	*Metric*
1 package dry yeast	7 grams
1/2 cup warm water	120 ml
1 tablespoon oil	15 ml
1/2 teaspoon salt	5 grams
2 cups flour, unsifted	280 grams
1 small can Italian tomato sauce, 8 oz	226.4 grams
2 tablespoons oregano	30 grams
4 oz Parmesan cheese	100 grams
8 oz mozzarella cheese, sliced or grated	200 grams
Optional (sausage, mushrooms, and ground beef)	

METHOD

Dissolve yeast in 1/2 cup of warm water. Place flour and salt in large bowl. Add the yeast mixture and mix well with the wooden spoon.

Turn dough out on floured board and knead for 15 minutes.

Place dough in clean bowl. Oil the surface of the dough and cover with wax paper and saran wrap. Cover loosely so there is room for the dough to rise. Let it rest in the bowl and then set it in the refrigerator overnight. The dough should double in size within the bowl.

NEXT DAY: Punch down and knead dough. Divide the dough into two sections. Roll each one out until it is the size of your pizza pan. Place in pan.

Cover with a small amount of olive oil, 1/2 can Italian tomato sauce, 1 tablespoon oregano, 1 small (8 oz) mozzarella cheese sliced thin or grated, 2 tablespoons Paremsan cheese, and add sliced mushrooms and ground beef or sausage. Bake at 400° F (205° C) for 20 minutes.

Makes 1 large pizza or 2 small.

❧CANNOLI À LA SICILIANA

Ingredients (Cannoli)
Flour
Butter
Salt
Fruit juice
White wine vinegar
Oil for deep frying

Filling:
Whipped cream
Powdered sugar
Vanilla
Cocoa
Ricotta cheese (cottage cheese if ricotta is not available)
Chocolate shavings (optional)

Utensils
Large bowl
Flour sifter
Large sauce pan
Wooden spoon
Knife
Large skillet
Tongs or slotted spoon
Rolling pin
Measuring cups and spoons
Cannoli pipes (either purchased or 4-inch lengths cut from a broom handle)

RECIPE

Standard	Metric
1 cup flour	140 grams
1 tablespoon butter	15 grams
2 tablespoons powdered sugar	35 grams
1 teaspoon white wine vinegar	10 ml
3 tablespoons fruit juice (apple, pear, pineapple)	45 ml
1 cup oil for deep frying	240 ml
1 teaspoon salt	10 grams

Filling:

1 cup whipped cream	240 ml
3 tablespoons powdered sugar	45 grams
1 teaspoon vanilla	5 ml
1 1/2 cups ricotta cheese	375 grams
3 tablespoons cocoa	35 grams
1/2 cup chocolate shavings	125 grams

(Ricotta cheese, a thick creamy cheese with no curds is similar to cottage cheese and may be found in the cheese section in most markets.)

METHOD

Sift the flour and powdered sugar into a large bowl. Add salt, melted butter, fruit juice, and vinegar. Stir well with a wooden spoon until the ingredients are well blended.

Knead well on a floured board for 5 minutes. Let the dough rest for 1/2 hour. Roll on floured board with rolling pin. Roll until the dough is a very thin sheet. Cut into four-inch squares.

Wrap dough diagonally around cannoli pipes that have been slightly greased. Fold dough points securely over one another so they don't separate when they are cooking. A little water on a finger will help when securing the dough.

Place enough oil in a skillet so that it is 1 1/2 inches deep. The cannolis will be deep fried. This whole operation should be done very carefully. Have a lid to the pan nearby or preferably a box of soda. Oil that is too hot could burst into flames. If it does, quickly smother the fire with the lid of the pan or baking soda, not water.

You can test the heat of the oil by dropping a small piece of batter into it. If it turns a golden color within a minute, three or four cannolis may be dropped into the hot oil and cooked. When they are golden, take them out with a slotted spoon or tongs and place on a paper towel to drain. When they are cool, gently remove from the cannoli pipes and continue frying more cannolis. Meanwhile, TURN OFF THE HEAT UNDER THE OIL. Only reheat the oil when you are ready to use it at that moment.

For the filling, whip the cream in a bowl with electric mixer until stiff. Place ricotta in another bowl, fold in whipped cream with rubber spatula or low speed of mixer. Add sugar, vanilla, and cocoa. Blend well.

The filling may be made earlier and chilled ready for use. Fill the cannolis shortly before serving, with a spatula or knife. Dip each end of cannoli into chocolate shavings.

Yield: 12–16.

A windmill in the countryside of Criptana.

Spanish National Tourist Department.

❧10❧
Paella and Pão-de-Lo

Don Quixote, the confused knight-errant of Spain, saw thirty giants with enormous arms. They were standing side by side on the plains of La Mancha. Despite the warnings of his "squire," Sancho Panza, he spurred his poor horse on at a furious gallop. He rushed upon one, only to break his lance in one of the "arms" which lifted him high in the air before dumping him at its feet. Of course, the "arms" were the sails of a windmill that was built to grind wheat kernels, not to vanquish a gentleman possessed by a dream of glory and chivalry.

Some of the windmills still stand on the treeless plains in central Spain where wheat is cultivated as it was in the day of the author of *Don Quixote*, Cervantes. Oxen pull the plow and donkeys thresh the grain by walking over and over it on stone floors. Wooden images of Don Quixote, who has been immortalized in story and song, stand in many shops in Madrid or other Spanish cities to tempt the tourists. Sometimes the faithful Sancho is carved to accompany his master. Sancho, it is written, devoured a stew of calves feet and onions, bacon, and turnips. The *cocida* of today is made from a variety of meats and vegetables and served with fresh, crusty bread. It may be found slowly cooking in the kitchens of both wealthy and poor.

Spain, itself, is a kind of melting pot of various peoples. We are apt to think only of the United States when we use the

Honoré Daumier, "Don Quixote and Sancho Panza." *The Metropolitan Museum of Art, Rogers Fund, 1972.*

term, but it may be applied to every European country, and especially Spain.

Once there was a land bridge between North Africa and the Spanish peninsula. The Iberians crossed over to clear fields and herd animals (the Basques in the Pyrenees Mountains may be their descendants). The Celts came next. Then the Greeks established ports in Spain and Portugal on the west coast. The capital of Portugal, Lisbon, was visited by Ulysses. Likewise, the Phoenicians, who brought the garbanzo bean, were ousted by the Romans, who made Spain their wheat granary and a source of olive oil. The Vandals, a Germanic tribe, pushed the Romans out, and they in turn were pushed into the north by

144

the Moors from North Africa, who brought the sugar cane and rice and the sweet orange. No other country in Europe grew sugar for well over 200 years.

It was Isabella of the province of Castile and her husband, Ferdinand of Aragon, who united all the Spanish provinces and drove the Moors out of the land. Spain became the richest country in the world. It was she who sent the Italian, Christopher Columbus, on the voyage in search of the spices and luxuries of the Orient. Instead, as we know, he found the New World, and it was not long before the Spanish flag flew over

Harvesting sugar cane in Motril, Granada. *Spanish National Tourist Department.*

territories that are now California, Mexico, Central America, Chile, Venezuela, and Peru in South America as well as the West Indies and the Philippines. Spanish conquistadors brought back crops that were to be worth far more than the luxuries of the Orient—even more than the gold that they obtained by ruthless conquest.

Everywhere that explorers landed in the Americas they noticed a new grain, corn, as it was cultivated by the Indians. As we shall learn when we study the grains of the United States, it proved to be one of the most valuable cereals with a very interesting story. Other new foods were taken to the Old World from America. Squash, pumpkins, tomatoes, potatoes, and peppers were cultivated in the terraced gardens of the Incas in Peru before their civilization was destroyed by the Spanish explorer, Pizarro.

In Mexico, Cortez and his small band of Spanish invaders were royally entertained in the palace of Montezuma, the Aztec emperor. Accustomed, himself, to drinking at least 50 pitchers a day of a cold drink made from chocolate and vanilla, he offered some of the frothy beverage with pastries made from cornmeal to his guests. The new drink was taken back to Spain where it became very popular, served hot and sweetened. Vanilla beans and chocolate from the cocoa bean were soon used as a flavoring for cakes in other parts of Europe. For a time, potatoes were fashionable; later they kept the poor alive. The Spaniards introduced Europe to turkeys and a method of barbecuing meat.

Spain is not a rich country now. Many millions of acres are planted in wheat, but the yield is not as large as it should be because modern methods of cultivation are not used. Wheat and grazing lands are on the central plains around the capital, Madrid. It is dry in the summer, but the rainfall is heavy in

Procession in Seville during Holy Week. Drawing by Domenico Gnoli, *Holiday* Magazine. *New York Public Library, Picture Collection.*

the winter months, thus ensuring a fairly good crop of winter wheat.

Bordering the Mediterranean, Barcelona is near a land of orange groves, olive trees, and fields of crocuses that are grown for a spice called saffron. Rice grows in marshy lands near the rivers. A specialty of the area is *paella*, made of fresh shellfish, chicken, and rice, seasoned with saffron and cooked outdoors in an especially wide, shallow pan that is placed on a tripod over a charcoal fire.

It is amazing that the Spanish people are as slim as they are, because they eat five meals a day. The first, a light breakfast, called *desayuno*, consists of cocoa and bread. Around 11 o'clock they have a more substantial meal of eggs and a sandwich and some sausage. Then they have a siesta. Stores close and all work stops. By 2 or 3 o'clock they are ready for a heavy meal, *la comida*. As in America, it starts with a salad, followed by a meat course, and a fruit for dessert. At six, they have a pastry or bread and coffee, and they eat again sometime between 9 and midnight. The last meal is a little lighter. It is called *la cena*. Shops are always open until 9 in the evening.

In Portugal, a small country on the western side of the Iberian Peninsula, three meals are served each day. As in most of Europe, breakfast consists of hot coffee with milk and bread. Because it is a land of fishermen, fish is served with lunch and dinner. The food is seasoned lightly with garlic and spices. Vegetables are well cooked and flavored. Sweets and pastry are popular.

The Portuguese are very courteous and hospitable. Should anyone enter their home at mealtime, the greeting would always be "Ladies and Gentlemen, you are served." They would even share their simple meal if you merely stopped to ask them directions by the roadside.

Every inch of this small country is carefully tilled by the hoe. It is a nation of small farms where corn is cultivated with beans and cabbage growing beside it to make the best use of

Breads of Portugal. Tall tray used in processions during Festival of the
Trays in Tomar.   *Heyward Associates, Inc.*

149

the available space. Rice is cultivated on the wet lowlands of the coast.

It was a Portuguese, Magellan, who first sailed around the world in 1520. Riches poured into Lisbon, the capital of Portugal, after Vasco da Gama found a new route to India, and the Portuguese colonized new settlements in the Orient, Africa, and the New World. Although their heritage is similar to Spain's, they broke away from Spanish domination in the seventeenth century.

The Portuguese love sweets. Even their traditional bread contains more sugar than the average loaf. Especially well liked are the light, fluffy, sponge cakes made of butter, several eggs, flour, sugar, and lemon flavoring. They are made in many sizes and shapes. A cake made in the shape of a ring is given to children at parties celebrating Epiphany or Three Kings Day on January 6. Trinkets and a single dried bean are placed within the cake before it is baked. The boy or girl who receives the bean is crowned King before the guests, who also share gifts with one another.

Likewise, in Spain the children eagerly await the coming of Epiphany. The night before, their shoes are carefully filled with grain and straw and placed on their doorsteps to provide food for the horses of the Three Kings of the East. The next morning, they discover gifts and sweets beside their empty shoes. The following recipe is one example of a Spanish type of sweet pastry that might be found by a happy child.

Rosquillas / *Spain*

Pastries are consumed in the late afternoon in Spain after the siesta. Because until recently ovens were rare in Spain, the pastries were more often fried in olive oil and sprinkled with sugar and pulverized almonds than baked. Rosquillas may be fried or baked, according to your preference.

Ingredients
All-purpose flour
Sugar
Vanilla
Egg
Butter
Olive oil (if fried
  in skillet)
Baking powder
Powdered sugar

Utensils
Measuring cups and spoons
Bowls
Wooden spoon
Rolling pin
Cookie sheet or skillet
Flour sifter

RECIPE

Standard	*Metric*
1 1/2 cups all-purpose flour	210 grams
1/3 cup sugar	80 grams
1 egg	
1 1/2 teaspoons baking powder	7 grams
1/4 teaspoon vanilla	5 ml
2 tablespoons butter, softened	30 grams

METHOD

Sift flour into bowl; add sugar, egg, baking powder, vanilla, and softened butter. Mix well with wooden spoon. Let the dough rest for 15 minutes in a warm place. Form a thin cord of dough about the size of your middle finger and three inches long. Form a circle with the strip of dough the size of a silver dollar. Repeat until all of the dough is used up. Makes about 18–20 small cakes.

The cakes may be placed on a greased cookie sheet and baked 15–20 minutes in a 350° F (177° C) oven, or fried in olive oil (about 1/2 cup in a skillet) until they are brown on one side, then turned and fried on the other (4 minutes per side).

Sprinkle powdered sugar over the hot cakes and serve warm.

❧PORTUGUESE SWEET BREAD

Miss Margaret Enas recalls the delicious bread her mother made in her home near Visalia, California. Several Portuguese families own large ranches in that area. The recipe has been cut in half to make three small loaves.

Ingredients	*Utensils*
Yeast	Measuring cups and spoons
Water	Bowls
Sugar	Rotary eggbeater
Butter	Sauce pan
Flour, all-purpose	3 small bread loaf tins
Milk	(3x4x3)
Eggs	
Lemon flavoring	
Salt	

RECIPE

Standard	*Metric*
1 package dry yeast	7 grams
2 tablespoons warm water	30 ml
2 eggs	
3/4 cups sugar	180 grams
1/2 stick (1/4 cup) +	
2 tablespoons butter	155 grams
1/2 cup milk scalded	120 ml
3 1/2 cups all-purpose	
flour (sifted)	450 grams
1 teaspoon lemon flavoring	5 ml
1/2 teaspoon salt	2 1/2 grams

METHOD

Bring milk to simmering point in a sauce pan. Melt butter in another sauce pan. Beat eggs well in medium-sized bowl with electric mixer or rotary eggbeater. Add sugar and salt. Beat for 15 minutes. Add warm milk, yeast mixture to beaten eggs and sugar. Stir in one-half of the flour and stir with wooden spoon until ingredients are well blended. Add remaining flour. Add melted butter and lemon flavoring.

Knead the dough for 15–20 minutes on a floured board. The longer you knead, the better. Place dough in large bowl. Put in a warm place to rise until it has doubled in size. Then shape into three small loaves in the bread tins.

Let rise again until doubled in size. Bake at 350° F (177° C) for 20–25 minutes.

Serves 6.

❧ PÃO-DE-LAO / A Portuguese Sponge Cake

This is a moist cake that is a brilliant yellow because it consists of many egg yolks in proportion to the amount of flour. It may be flavored with vanilla, lemon, or cinnamon.

Ingredients	*Utensils*
Eggs	Rotary eggbeater or electric
Lemon flavoring, vanilla,	mixer
or cinnamon	Measuring cups and spoons
Flour	Small cake pans
Sugar	Cooling rack
Salt	Wax paper

RECIPE

Standard	*Metric*
4 egg yolks	
1 whole egg	
1/2 teaspoon salt	3 grams
1/3 cup sugar	80 grams
2 tablespoons cake flour	30 grams
1 teaspoon vanilla or lemon flavoring, or 1/2 teaspoon cinnamon	3–4 grams

METHOD

Beat the egg and yolks with beater until they are very light and frothy. Use high speed on electric beater. Beat 15 minutes with rotary eggbeater. Gradually add sugar while beating. Add flour and salt, beat two more minutes. Add flavoring.

Turn into small cake pan (six inches in width) that has been buttered and lined with wax paper. Bake in a low oven, 325° F (163° C) for 50 minutes. Cool on rack with pan turned upside down.

Serves 4.

PAELLA

Ingredients	Utensils
Olive oil	Large skillet
Onion	Knife
Garlic	Measuring spoons and cups
Cut-up frying chicken	Wooden spoon
Sliced ham	Bowl
Shrimp	Lid for skillet
Tomatoes	Skillet or an electric
Rice	frying pan
Saffron	
Salt and pepper	
Clams	
Clear chicken broth	
Peas	
Pimento	

RECIPE

Standard	Metric
2 tablespoons olive oil	30 ml
1 onion, finely chopped	125 grams
1 clove garlic, chopped	50 grams

1 small cut-up fryer (2–3 lbs)	1000–1500 grams
1 cup chopped ham	240 grams
1/2 lb shrimp	
(shelled and deveined)	226 grams
6 sliced tomatoes	453 grams
1 cup uncooked rice	240 grams
1/4 teaspoon saffron	2 grams
1 teaspoon salt	5 grams
1 teaspoon pepper	5 grams
6 clams (6 oz)	170 grams
2 cups peas	286 grams
1 (10 3/4 oz)can clear	
chicken broth	305 grams
1/2 cup sliced pimento	125 grams

METHOD

Heat the oil in the skillet. Sauté the chicken until it is golden. Place the chicken aside in a bowl. Sauté shrimp and ham in same oil used for chicken. Remove to a bowl with chicken.

Sauté the onion and then the garlic in the skillet. Add tomatoes, chicken broth, saffron, salt, and pepper. Bring to a boil and add the rice. Simmer 5 minutes. Add peas, clam juice, and clams and simmer 5 more minutes. Arrange the shrimp, chicken, and ham over the rice mixture. Cover and cook for 5–10 minutes, until all the broth has been absorbed. Garnish with pimento strips and cook 5 more minutes. Remove from stove. Set aside for 5–10 minutes and serve in skillet.

Serves 6.

❧11❧
Crepes and Quiches

The fine cooking of Europe reached its peak in the palace of Versailles near Paris. Known as "haute cuisine," it is a skillful blending of the best culinary traditions of the kitchens of the peasants and kings. Chefs who had received their training in Paris rose to the importance of men of privilege. They were in great demand throughout the world. President Thomas Jefferson secured the services of one named Lemaire and brought him to the United States.

However, their job was not easy. A meal was considered a work of art, and a small dinner required a great deal of preparation. At Versailles, banquets were splendid affairs. Vatel, who was in charge of the royal kitchens, was required to prepare at least one banquet per day for five thousand guests. On one unfortunate day the fish that he ordered did not arrive on time. Feeling his honor and reputation were ruined, he committed suicide. He obviously, like Apicius, took food too seriously.

The French have always taken their food seriously. When a small tribe of Celts, called the Parisii, settled in the middle of an island on the Seine River because they were safe there from the wolves of the dense forests, they were even then interested in the taste of their food. The Romans who conquered them wrote of the large amount of meat they ate with a little

Ball supper in Galerie de Diane, at the Tuileries (Paris). *Illustrated News,* 1869 (London). *New York Public Library, Picture Collection.*

bread. They adopted one of the Parisii's favorite dishes, milk-fed snails. They are called *escargots* today. The Romans brought wheat to France and it was not long before water mills along the Seine were grinding the grain that grew so well north of Paris. Among nations, France ranks fifth as a producer of wheat, which, along with wine grapes, are their leading crops. Additional supplies of wheat need to be imported because of the French people's fondness for white bread.

France is a flour and butter country. The French are very adept in combining them with seasonings and herbs, milk or meat juices. They were well-known for sauces that were invented to restore flavor to meat that requires a long period of cooking. Beef is not as tender in Europe as it is in the United States. It requires long slow cooking.

Grain cultivation by the peasants and making bread from oats and barley; facsimile of an engraving out of the wood of Virgil.
From *Moeurs, Usages et Costumes au Moyen Age et à L'Epoque de la Renaissance* by Paul La Croix. Paris, 1872. *New York Public Library, Picture Collection.*

French cooking is indebted to the cuisine of other lands as well as its own. It all began when Catherine De Medici brought her chefs from Florence when she married a French king. New recipes, new vegetables, ice cream, and fillet steaks were introduced to the French court. Then La Varenne, a court chef, published a cookbook in 1651 that gave the people excellent directions for the preparation of the French-Italian cuisine that evolved. He also recommended saving the juice from meats that required long cooking and mixing them with bread crumbs and delicate seasoning to restore flavor to the meat. Soon flour and butter replaced the bread crumbs. Later, Marie Antoinette, to her eventual misfortune, married a

158

Distribution of bread during the scarcity of 1709. From an old engraving. From
Le Magasin Pittoresque, Paris, 1842.   *New York Public Library, Picture
Collection.*

French prince who became King Louis XVI. As a wedding present, her mother and father, the rulers of Austria at Vienna, gave her pastry cooks and special kitchens for her new home at Versailles, where she played games of being a milkmaid or a shepherdess to lessen her boredom with life at court. Supposedly it was she who said "Let them have cake" when she heard that the people had no bread.

The starving people were forced to fill what bread they had with earth to make it more filling. Soon feasting courts and starving peasants resulted in the bloody French Revolution. The court life was eliminated but an obsession with fine eating and cooking did not end with the Revolution. Chefs of the old courts opened restaurants in Paris, which began to number in the hundreds.

Pastries became a work of art. Salads, which always follow the main course, were carefully constructed. Alexander Dumas, famous for many exciting books, such as *The Three Musketeers* and *The Count of Monte Cristo*, was most proud of his *Dictionary of Cooking*. He spent a lifetime on it, while the others were written for a profit that he spent on food.

Napoleon, who was not a gourmet, offered a prize of 12,000 francs to anyone who could invent a method of preserving food for his armies. Thus, canning of fruits and vegetables began. Pasteur, another famous Frenchman, saved the lives of many children by working out a process to kill germs in milk, which became known as pasteurization.

Peasants realized the fulfillment of their dreams after the Revolution. They became small landowners with one or two fields to cultivate and a few cows, goats, and a vegetable garden. They produced enough food for themselves and did not mind the hard work because they were attached to their land with a kind of reverence. Some of the best French recipes came from peasant kitchens.

Until World War I, France was able to produce enough wheat for its entire population. That required quite a bit of

Model Bakery for the Public Audience. Oven and mechanical kneading room. *Bettmann Archive.*

wheat, as many loaves of delicious crusty bread are baked daily in village bakeries. The bakers have retained their trade secrets and have special ovens. Sometimes a member of a family will shop for bread three times a day. Boys and girls bring it home on their bicycles after school.

Then two wars ravaged the countryside. Their cattle, their fields, their machinery and tools were destroyed. Many went to the cities to work in factories after the war, and there were not enough people to till the soil. Some labor was imported,

Modern Bakery.   *French Embassy Press and Information Division.*

but they were not as interested in work as the small farmer who owns his own land. Still about one out of every five Frenchmen is a farmer who lives in a village surrounded by farmland. They do not live on their farms as we do. Nor are the plots that they own adjacent to one another. They leave their village home each day and go out to the fields, first to one and then to another, perhaps a mile away from the first. The government is attempting to remedy this situation by reassembling the land. Also cooperatives are being formed that will allow communities to obtain and share expensive machinery. Generally, the farmer prefers the old-fashioned methods of tilling the soil, although he does interchange wheat with clover and alfalfa to replenish it.

162

The day begins rather early in France. Factories and shops open around seven in the morning. Most of the grocery shopping is done in the morning as soon as the children are in school. Although food may be purchased in shops in Paris, there are many outside markets in many districts. In every village there are two market days a week when fresh produce is sold. The prices may not be better than a supermarket, but the Frenchwoman feels that the fruits and vegetables are fresher. She buys her bread and pastries at one store, her meat at another, and so on. She prefers to cook the food long and slowly. She may begin in the morning for the preparation of the evening meal, unless, of course, she lives in an apartment in Paris and works in a shop. Then she stops at the supermarket as we do in America and resorts to some prepared food. Almost everyone prefers to make his own dressing for a salad that is an essential part of the meal. The preparation of a meal is very important—it must be as attractive and pleasant as possible.

Children have a snack of bread and butter or bread and jam after school. Sometimes they purchase a pastry or an ice cream on the way home. Ice cream is sold from portable carts that can be pushed along the sidewalks. It is lighter than ours, more like ice milk.

Mantes (Seine-et-Oise): Wheat harvesting.
French Embassy Press and Information Division.

Most of the Europeans have a plain roll and coffee for breakfast. For a special treat they enjoy a croissant, a delicious and feathery roll that the French make so well. Actually, the first croissant was made in Budapest in 1686. The Turks who were attacking the city had built underground passages to reach the center of town. Their plan was foiled by bakers working at night. They heard the Turks and immediately gave the alarm, thus saving the city. The next day they went back to their bakeries and made rolls of the same shape as the crescent on the Turkish flag. Crescent rolls, or croissants as the French call them, became popular throughout Europe and especially in France. Most French cookbooks include a recipe for making them. As they are difficult, they should only be attempted by an accomplished baker.

However, there are so many French treats that are not at all difficult to prepare. They are well worth the small amount of effort required. Some may seem very familiar.

Crepes

In Brittany they say that Anne, who was the daughter of the Duke of Brittany, created the first crepe to provide food for a royal party accompanying the King of France. All that she had was a bit of flour and milk and perhaps an egg. Her work was well rewarded because she became Queen of France one year later in 1491. The king's reward was the Duchy of Brittany.

Now a part of the Republic of France, the Department of Brittany, situated on the eastern shore of the English Channel, is considered the home of the French crepe. The Bretons still love the old stories and traditions about themselves. They say that King Arthur was born in Brittany. Although they are decidedly French, they are the descendants of people who fled the Saxons when they invaded England. They speak a Gaelic

164

language that is similar to the Welsh language among themselves, although French is their official language.

Crepes and apple cider are a daily delight in the villages in the province of Brittany. Children purchase them in the market squares on their way home from school. They generally buy them from a portable creperie that has been built on the back of a truck. The crepes are made on a large black griddle that has been placed over a gas flame. The children fold them into halves or quarters, sprinkle a little sugar or spread jam and butter on them, and eat them warm from the griddle.

A wooden tool, called a *recletta*, is deftly used to spread the batter into a large circle. It is a flat piece of wood attached to a dowel or handle and is quickly turned around in a clockwise direction, as a compass, to draw a circle. The crepe is turned with a pancake turner to bake one more minute. Butter is spread over the top before it is folded. Paper thin crepes became the vogue in Paris, where they are made of fine white flour and baked in a six- or seven-inch crepe pan. The idea spread into other European countries. They are becoming popular in the United States either as a dessert filled with fruit or ice cream topped with whipped cream and chocolate or as a main course of a luncheon or dinner. In that case the fillings are delicious combinations of meat and vegetables or creamed fish. You can use your imagination. The following recipe may be made in a small crepe pan, Paris fashion, or on a large griddle with a recletta, Brittany style. A simple entrée (main course) filling is included. Brittany crepes are large if made properly but they, too, may be filled. They need not be turned. Both methods require a bit of practice but the result is well worth it. The crepe-pan method is a little easier.

CREPES

Ingredients	**Utensils**
Flour	Bowl
Milk and water	Measuring spoons and cups
Egg	Wooden spoon or blender
Butter or vegetable oil	Soup ladle
Sugar	Crepe pan and rubber
Vanilla	spatula or 7-inch griddle
Orange juice or fruit juice	(large griddle and recletta
	if you wish to make them as
	they do in Brittany)

RECIPE
(Makes 1 1/4 cups [300 ml]. Recipe may be doubled.)

Standard	**Metric**
1/2 cup flour	70 grams
1/2 cup milk	120 ml
1/4 cup water	60 ml
1 egg	
1 teaspoon oil or butter	5 ml
2 tablespoons sugar	30 grams
1/2 teaspoon vanilla	3 ml
1 tablespoon orange juice for	
flavoring	15 ml

METHOD
Crepe batter should be very thin, like cream. Place the ingredients in the bowl in the order given, mixing continually. *Refrigerate* for at least two hours, but no longer than 24 hours. If you wish to use the batter within a short time, it may be made in a blender, but it should be refrigerated at least 1/2 hour so that the flour will absorb the liquid.

Now consider the first two or three practice crepes:
1. Preheat the pan on medium heat. There are many crepe pans on the market, but a 6- or 7-inch skillet will do. Never

use the pan for anything but crepes and clean it with salt and oil. Never wash it in water.

2. For your convenience, have within reach a hot pad, a serving spoon or ladle, a rubber spatula, and the bowl of batter. The skillet has been preheated and will be ready for use when a drop of water will sizzle and bounce. Place a little oil on a paper towel and grease the griddle.

3. Remove the skillet or pan from the fire. Place a small amount of batter in the bottom of the pan. (I fill the ladle 1/2 full.) Roll the pan around until the batter covers the bottom and reaches up the sides. Don't try to fill up any holes that might appear. Pour off the excess batter into the bowl. Return the pan to the heat and bake the crepe about two minutes. The edges should be slightly brown and the batter set.

4. Now the crepe is carefully turned. Use whatever method is best for you. A rubber spatula may be used to turn the crepe or you may need to do it as I do. Lift the edges slightly with the spatula. Pick up the crepe carefully with your fingers, and quickly place the unbaked side down on the pan. Bake a minute longer until the crepe does not sizzle. Remove with a spatula. The crepes should be stacked for later use. They may be wrapped and frozen. Do not place paper in between each crepe. They will separate nicely when they have thawed.

Remember the crepe should be so thin that you can see the pattern when you place it on a plate!

ENTRÉE CREPE FILLING

Ingredients	*Utensils*
Crepes made previously	Sauce pan
Boiled sliced ham	Ovenproof baking dish
Asparagus	Knife
Sauce Bechamel or Sauce	Tongs or slotted spoon
Mornay (recipes follow)	Large spoon

RECIPE

Standard   *Metric*
10 previously cooked crepes
10 slices boiled ham, packaged
    at market
1 lb asparagus, or 2 bunches   450 grams

METHOD

Cut off and discard the tough ends of the asparagus. Wash remaining stems and heads. Tie together with string and stand
them in a deep sauce pan. Fill with water to within one inch of
the heads. Boil for 25 minutes uncovered. Remove from water
with tongs or slotted spoon. Drain.

Spread out the crepes. Cover each with one ham slice. Place
2–3 stalks of asparagus on each slice of ham. Roll crepes, ham,
and asparagus together. Place all 10 in an ovenproof dish. Bake
in hot oven 400° F (205° C) for 15 minutes.

Meanwhile make white sauce (Sauce Bechamel) or Sauce
Mornay from the following recipe. Cover each crepe with 2
spoonfuls of sauce before serving with salad of your choice.

Serves 5.

SAUCE BECHAMEL

Sauce Bechamel is simply a white sauce made of flour, butter,
milk, and seasoning. It should not be made long before it is
used.

A *roux* is a mixture of flour and butter that has been cooked
for a minute in a skillet. It is the basis of a *white sauce*, as
Sauce Bechamel is called in most American cookbooks. It is
used for creamed fish or vegetables.

Ingredients   *Utensils*
Flour   Skillet
Butter   Measuring spoon and cups

168

Milk   Wooden spoon
Seasoning (salt, pepper, or
    celery salt, onion salt, and
    nutmeg)

RECIPE

Standard	Metric
1 tablespoon flour	15 grams
1 tablespoon butter	15 grams
1 cup milk	240 ml
Seasoning — 1/4 teaspoon each of salt and pepper, according to taste	1 1/4 grams

METHOD

Make *roux* by melting butter in skillet. Take it off the heat and add the flour. Return to low heat and cook for one minute, stirring constantly with wooden spoon. Gradually add the milk and continue to stir. Add seasoning. Cook until sauce thickens — about 2 minutes. Stir constantly with wooden spoon to prevent scorching.

SAUCE MORNAY

Make a white sauce as above. Use 1/2 teaspoon mustard (1 gram), 2 tablespoons of grated Cheddar cheese, and 2 tablespoons (6 grams each) of grated Swiss cheese instead of spice seasoning.

Quiche Lorraine

Alsace and Lorraine are two French provinces that border the Rhine River. They have been traded back and forth between France and Germany as a result of several wars between the two countries. Lorraine is the home of the very fine cheese pie, Quiche Lorraine. Originally it was a German dish called *kuchen*, the German word for pie or cake. The French people could not pronounce it; it sounds like *quiche* to them.

The following recipe for Quiche Lorraine was given to me by the excellent chef and owner of the restaurant La Mere Michelle in Saratoga, California. Expertly trained in Europe for his profession, he began his career on the Orient Express.

QUICHE LORRAINE

Ingredients	*Utensils*
Pastry shell:	Quiche pan or pie tin
Flour	Flour sifter
Salt	Knife
Butter	Rolling pin
Vegetable shortening	Rotary egg beater
Egg	Bowl
Milk	Measuring cups and spoons
	Cheese grater
Filling:	Griddle for frying bacon
Bacon	A quiche pan (similar to a
Eggs	pie pan but the sides are
Flour	straight and fluted.)
Cream, half and half	
Nutmeg	
Salt	
Gruyere cheese	
Emmenthaler cheese	

One may substitute American Swiss cheese obtainable in any market, although the effect is not quite as pleasing as the imported Swiss cheeses. Gruyere and Emmenthaler are obtainable in specialty shops and food stores that deal in imports. Also chopped ham may be substituted for bacon.

RECIPE

Standard
2 cups flour

Metric
260 grams

170

1 teaspoon salt	5 grams
1 stick butter	125 grams
2 tablespoons shortening	30 ml
1 egg	
3 tablespoons milk	45 ml

Filling:

8 strips of bacon, broiled and set aside	
3 whole eggs	
1 egg yolk	
1 tablespoon flour	15 grams
Pinch of salt and nutmeg	3 grams each
2 cups half and half cream	480 ml
1 tablespoon melted butter	30 grams
6 oz of each cheese or	188 grams
12 oz of American Swiss	

METHOD

Sift 2 cups of flour into bowl. Add salt, butter cut into small chunks, and the shortening. Mix well and add beaten egg and 3 tablespoons of milk. Work to a paste with your hands. Let it rest five minutes.

Roll out dough on a floured board with rolling pin. Fit into 9-inch pie pan or quiche pan. Set it in the refrigerator until you are ready to use it.

Beat in a bowl the whole eggs and egg yolk. Add flour, pinch of nutmeg and salt, and cream. Shred the cheese on cheese grater. Add with 1 tablespoon of melted butter to egg and cream mixture. Place bacon strips over pie crust like wagon wheel spokes. Pour the egg and cheese mixture over the bacon.

Set pie pan on cookie sheet. Bake in 375° F (191° C) oven for 35–45 minutes. May be served hot or cold.

Serves 4–6.

❧12❧
Smorgasbord and Smorrebrod

The Boy Scouts of Denmark have completed a noteworthy project. Aided by archeological discoveries, they have reproduced an old Viking village at New Hedeby, Denmark. The homes are replicas of the dwelling places of their ancestors. They have thatch or sod roofs, sides of white-washed wattle (mud) held in place by wooden beams. Some of the scouts have built a ship by using the old methods and tools. Thirty-two young men row with all of their strength as they swiftly glide over the North Sea as the Vikings did in the year 787 A.D. and for a good two hundred and fifty years thereafter.

The Vikings were excellent navigators who brought terror to much of Europe when they plundered and traded or sought new lands to settle. They were unsuccessful in their attack upon Paris, because they were unable to pass the armed bridges from the main island to the banks of the Seine River. They ruled in England for a time, were given French Normandy, were the first rulers in Russia, harassed ports on the Mediterranean, and even journeyed as far as the east coast of North America. They followed the same polar route that airplanes now take from America to Europe. It is hard to imagine

From the Annual Viking Festival at Frederikssund.

Danish National Travel Office.

anyone having enough courage to navigate on these waters even in a modern steamship, much less a hundred-foot-long "Dragon Ship."

For a long time the farmers were content in their home in the north and only ventured forth to sea for fish. They lived together in long houses. A fireplace in the center kept them warm during the long winters. Their kitchens were well supplied with iron pots and pans and attractive pottery bowls. They ate fish, game, and meat, oats and barley porridge, and rye bread with knives and spoons, but no forks. They grew some apples, nuts, and onions. Since wheat needs a longer growing season for ripening than is afforded in the far north, thin crops of rye and barley had to suffice. A fondness for rye bread still lingers in all of the Scandinavian countries. However, Sweden has fertile soil in the south that lends itself well to the cultivation of wheat. Enough is grown for Sweden with a surplus to sell to Germany. Oats and barley are important in Norway, but wheat must be imported. The Finns grow more rye than any other grain.

Denmark is one of the best examples of a nation that has surmounted difficulties. A small country with unpredictable weather and only fair soil, its profits from grain were wiped out eighty years ago because of increased competition in the rest of the world. But Danish farmers had the Viking fighting spirit and met the challenge with imagination and scientific research.

Today three-fourths of the land is devoted to agriculture. Small farms dot a neat and charming landscape. A portion of each farm is devoted to barley, rye, and oats, and some wheat that alternates with sugar beets. The remaining fields are devoted to grazing land. Grain is imported for the livestock that has made Denmark the champion exporter of bacon, butter, cheese, and eggs. Each farmer owns his land. He is also a member of a cooperative that enables him to share in the use of expensive machinery, and to acquire more scientific infor-

Grain being harvested with the help of a combine in Nysted, Denmark.

United Nations.

mation on plants and animals in order to reap a good profit from his carefully grown cereals and livestock.

He enjoys a breakfast of three kinds of light and dark bread with jam or cheese, either rye or white bread flavored with onion, cheese, or caraway seeds, and coffee. Lunch in the Scandinavian countries is an open-faced sandwich which is attractively served at home or in restaurants, on trains, or aboard the boats that journey up and down the fjords of Norway. Dinners are simple, unless company is invited. Then they are special. Always good hosts, the people love to share their home and food. Years ago the homemakers frequently kept a table of bread and butter prepared for an unexpected visitor or lonely wayfarer. The *smorgasbord*, which translates into bread and butter table, or *kold bord* (cold table) dates back to the Viking days when people traveled great distances to enjoy several days of feasting from a common table where all helped themselves and placed their food on a piece of bread rather than a plate. To help provide a lavish meal the guests brought cereals, fish, and game prepared according to their methods.

The custom was firmly established for entertaining in private

Great variety of open sandwiches in a 24-hour sandwich shop in Copenhagen. *Danish National Travel Office.*

homes during the seventeenth century, and the tradition spread to hotels and restaurants during the nineteenth century. Possibly it was a result of the building of railroads that brought people together in hotels and resorts for a holiday. One hotel, the Stalheim, nestled in the mountains and fjords of Norway, daily serves the most beautiful and lavish smorgasbord that one may imagine. Not far from the main railroad line between Oslo and Bergen, it is a main attraction for tourists from far distant places and a former retreat for the crowned heads of Europe.

Here, as is the custom, an established procedure is followed. A start is made with bread and butter and herring either pickled or plain. As a person proceeds around the table he helps himself to other types of fish—smoked salmon, shrimp, or lobster. Next in turn are egg dishes, salads, then cold meats and cheeses. The smorgasbord may be a prelude to the main dish of the meal, or it may include a variety of hot dishes, such as meatballs, potatoes, vegetables, fish, and a dessert of fresh fruit or cake. It is an ideal way of entertaining many people. Therefore it has become popular in other countries, especially the United States.

Midsummer Eve, or Saint John's Eve, on June 23 is celebrated in Denmark, Sweden, Norway, and Finland. Summer is beautiful and very welcome in the northern lands. Its beginning is celebrated with dancing, singing, and blazing bonfires. An old saying is:

As high as you jump over Saint John's bonfire,
so high will the grain grow the coming year.

When the midsummer fires that have been built on every height and shore have burned to dying embers, young people make a sport of jumping over the embers, or if lovers, they walk hand in hand in the adjacent forests. In many regions, a village girl is chosen as queen. She is crowned with a headpiece made of midsummer flowers. A village fiddler plays a traditional wedding march during the ceremony.

Saint Lucy's Day opens the Yule season. A young village girl is chosen to carry a candle and a tray filled with coffee and Lucia buns from house to house. Garbed in a long white dress with a crimson sash and crowned with a garland of leaves, the honored girl is frequently escorted by baker boys who assist her on calls. They carry trays filled with buns made from the following recipe. Raisins are placed on the buns to represent the eyes of Saint Lucy.

❧LUCIA BUNS / Swedish

Ingredients	Utensils
Flour, all-purpose	Double boiler
Milk	Bowl (large)
Sugar	Wooden spoon
Salt	Measuring cups and spoons
Yeast, dry	Cookie sheet
Egg	Wire rack
Raisins, seedless, dark	Spatula
Crushed cardamom seeds (optional)	
Margarine or butter	

RECIPE

Standard	Metric
3/4 cup milk	180 ml
1/3 cup sugar	80 grams
1 teaspoon salt	5 grams
1/4 cup or 1/2 stick butter	60 grams
1 teaspoon pulverized cardamom	5 grams
1/2 cup warm water	120 ml

2 packages dry yeast	14 grams
1 egg, beaten	
4–5 cups unsifted all-purpose flour	560–700 grams
1/2 cup raisins	100 grams

METHOD

Scald milk in double boiler; stir in sugar, salt, butter or margarine. Cool to lukewarm. Measure 1/2 cup warm water in large bowl. Add yeast and stir until dissolved. Add milk mixture, egg, cardamom, and 2 cups flour. Beat well with wooden spoon until dough is smooth. Stir in additional flour gradually. Turn out onto lightly floured board and knead 10 minutes. Place in greased bowl. Grease top of dough slightly. Let rise in warm place until double in bulk, about one hour.

Punch risen dough down. Let it rest 10 minutes. Divide into 18 equal pieces. Roll each into strip 12 inches long between hands. Cut in half. Place strips together to form an X on cookie sheet that has been greased.

Curl ends of strips. Place raisins in center of each curl. Bake 15 minutes at 350° F (177° C). Remove from cookie sheet with spatula. Cool on wire rack.

Finnish Farmer Rye Bread

Rye bread is the favorite of the Finns. The best thing a Finnish hostess can give to a guest is fresh harvest bread, made in the fall immediately after the harvest. Traditionally it was made twice a year because the huge outdoor ovens were difficult to heat. Strung on poles from the rafters, it nourished the people throughout the long winters. Made again in the spring to prepare for the summer's work, it was served with heavy soups, cereal porridges, milk and fruit, and fish from the sea and the many sparkling lakes of this beautiful country where the people are athletic and proud. They are greatly respected and admired because they tightened their belts and paid their war debts to us in spite of the ravaging of the land by Germany and Russia.

Rye is a grain that can grow in cold and damp climates. It resembles wheat but is much hardier and will grow in sandy soil, either planted in rows or scattered over the field.

The flour that is milled from rye is heavier than wheat. It was looked down upon by wheat eaters, probably because it was made into bread by the poor in central and northern Europe. It makes a darker and heavier loaf.

Until the beginning of the twentieth century, the Finns did not use wheat flour to make bread. Instead they used a sour dough made from rye and milk. The addition of wheat makes the dough more manageable, although sourdough is the preference of the Scandinavians. A recipe for both types will follow. Rye bread is the basis for the famous Scandinavian open-faced sandwich called *smorrebrod* in Danish.

FINNISH RYE BREAD

Ingredients	Utensils
Yeast	Measuring cups or spoons
Honey	Wooden spoon
Butter or margarine	Round 9-inch cake pan
Salt	Cooling rack
Rye flour	
All-purpose flour	

RECIPE

Standard	Metric
1 package dry yeast	7 grams
1/4 cup warm water	60 ml
1 cup lukewarm water	240 ml
1 1/2 tablespoons honey	22 grams

1 1/2 tablespoons melted butter or margarine	22 grams
1 1/2 teaspoons salt	7 grams
1 1/2 cups rye flour	240 grams
1 1/2 cups all-purpose flour	200 grams

METHOD

In a large bowl dissolve yeast in 1/4 cup warm water. Add the rest of the water, salt, honey, and butter when the yeast is slightly foamy (about 5 minutes). Add rye flour and beat. Stir in all-purpose flour.

Turn dough onto a heavily floured board. If a little more all-purpose flour is needed, work it in as you knead the dough. Knead for 10 minutes. Dough will be smooth and elastic and very manageable. Place in a greased bowl. Grease the top of the dough slightly. Cover with a towel, and set in a warm place until the dough has doubled in size.

Punch it down and knead 5 more minutes. Let rise again for 1 hour. Bake in a greased round pan in a preheated 350° F (177° C) oven for 1 hour.

A Finnish loaf is hard crusted. Cool on a wire rack before slicing.

SMORREBROD

Smorrebrod means bread and butter. Actually it refers to the Scandinavian open-faced sandwiches that are served at luncheons, after-theater parties, or late evening entertainment. Arranged attractively on large trays, they are works of art.

Made of interesting combinations of food, the basis is thinly sliced rye bread, generously buttered.

Try the following toppings:

1. Two thinly sliced pieces of salami, folded into cones. Let one overlap the other. Garnish with two thinly sliced onion rings and a sprig of parsley.

2. Cheese slices rolled and placed on the buttered bread. Garnish with thin slices of radish.
3. Liver paste, sliced mushrooms, and marinated cucumber slices.
   Cucumber: Slice as thin as possible. Let stand overnight in 1 cup of sugar mixed with 1/2 cup vinegar. Very fine tasting.
4. Tiny shrimp piled on a lettuce leaf. Garnish with a slice of lemon.
5. Strips of ham garnished with tomato and watercress.
6. Roast pork thinly sliced and garnished with a twisted slice of orange.
7. Roast beef and thin slice of pickle.

SOURDOUGH RYE BREAD

Ingredients	Utensils
Yeast	Large bowl
Milk	Wooden spoon
Warm water	2 bread loaf tins (4"x4"x6")
Salt	Cooling rack
Rye flour	Measuring cups and spoons
Whole wheat flour	Clean towel

RECIPE

Standard	Metric
Sourdough starter:	
1/2 cup rye flour	60 grams
1/2 cup milk	120 ml

Place in bowl and let it stand in warm place for two days. Cover with saran wrap or wax paper.

1/2 cup starter	
1 package yeast	7 grams
1 1/2 cups warm water	360 ml

1 1/2 teaspoons salt	7 grams
3 1/2 cups rye flour	600 grams
2 1/2 cups whole wheat flour	350 grams

METHOD

Place the yeast and 1/2 cup of water in a large bowl. After five minutes, add the sourdough starter. Add 1 1/2 cups warm water and salt. Stir well.

Add the rye flour and beat with wooden spoon. When the batter is well mixed, add the whole wheat flour, 1/2 cupful at a time.

Place dough on floured counter and knead for 10 minutes. Place in greased bowl, and let double in size in warm place after covering with towel. Take dough out of the bowl and knead it again for 5 minutes.

Divide dough into 2 loaves. Place in loaf tins. Let dough rise until it has doubled its size once more. Bake in hot oven that has been preheated to 400° F (205° C) for 45–50 minutes. Take out of loaf tin immediately and cool on rack. Slice and serve when cool.

Makes 2 loaves.

EBLESKIVERS

One of the national dishes of Denmark, they are unlike the pancakes of other countries. They are like a light and fluffy round ball and often contain a fruit center. Similar to a doughnut or fritter, they are made in a griddle that has seven cups or depressions on its surface. At least a tablespoon of oil is placed in each cup. The ebleskivers are turned with a fork or a pair of knitting needles. My friend, Inga, whose parents were born in Denmark, gave me her family recipe.

Ingredients	Utensils
Flour	Flour sifter
Baking powder	Rotary egg beater
Salt	Rubber spatula
Sugar	Bowl
Buttermilk	Measuring cups and spoons
Butter	Wooden spoon
Eggs	Sauce pan
	Ebleskiver pan (purchased in department stores or shops that specialize in kitchen wares)

RECIPE

Standard	Metric
2 cups flour	280 grams
2 teaspoons baking powder	10 grams
1 teaspoon salt	5 grams
2 tablespoons sugar	30 grams
2 cups buttermilk	480 ml
4 tablespoons melted butter	60 grams
4 eggs	
1/2 cup shortening for greasing skillet	125 ml

METHOD

Separate eggs and beat the egg whites in medium-size bowl until very stiff. Beat with a clean, dry rotary egg beater or whisk. In large bowl sift flour that has been presifted and measured once.

Melt butter in sauce pan. Add baking powder, salt, sugar, buttermilk, melted butter, and egg yolks to flour. Beat with a wooden spoon until the batter is smooth.

Fold in egg whites with rubber spatula. If necessary, add more egg whites to the batter after several ebleskivers have been made. Egg whites will make them light and fluffy.

Preheat ebleskiver pan on medium-hot heat. Place one tablespoon shortening in each cup in ebleskiver pan. Drop 5 tablespoons of batter into each cup. A thin piece of apple may be placed in each ebleskiver before it is turned. Cook until they are bubbly, then keep turning with fork or knitting needles until all sides are brown. Remove carefully with forks. Serve with butter and jam or powdered sugar.

Serves 8. Delicious!

SWEDISH PANCAKES

Plattar or Swedish pancakes are baked on an iron griddle called a *plattpanna*. The top of the griddle consists of seven flat depressions about three inches in diameter. They make a small, light, perfectly round pancake, more like a sponge cake than a crepe. Serve as a dessert with a topping of whipped cream and lingonberries (similar to cranberries) or strawberries. They may be baked on a plain griddle if the traditional Swedish griddle is not available.

Ingredients	*Utensils*
Eggs	Measuring cups, liquid and dry
Cream	Flour sifter
Flour	Sauce pan
Sugar	Rotary egg beater
Milk	Spatula
Butter or margarine	Bowl
Salt	Wooden spoon
Shortening for greasing skillet	
Whipped cream	
Lingonberries or strawberries	

RECIPE

(Courtesy of the Swedish Consulate in San Francisco)

Standard	*Metric*
3 eggs	
1 cup cream	240 ml
2 cups milk	480 ml
1 cup sifted flour	130 grams
1 tablespoon sugar	15 grams
1/4 cup melted butter	60 grams
1/4 teaspoon salt	2 grams
1 tablespoon shortening for greasing skillet	15 grams
1 cup whipped cream	240 grams
2 cups fruit (lingonberries or strawberries) or 1 cup jam	270 grams

METHOD

Beat the eggs and cream in a bowl with rotary egg beater. Sift flour and measure one cup. Add flour to the eggs and cream. Beat with wooden spoon or electric mixer until the batter is smooth. Slowly add milk, melted butter, sugar, and salt. Beat well.

Preheat griddle and drop 1/4–1/2 teaspoon shortening in each pan, or lightly grease entire American griddle. Drop 2 tablespoons batter in each section of Swedish plattpanna or same amount on American griddle. Be sure to make each pancake a 3-inch round. Turn with spatula when surface starts to bubble. It takes one minute or two until the other side is a golden brown. Remove with spatula.

Serve immediately or stack in aluminum foil. Reheat in oven before serving with berries or jam and a light whipped cream.

Serves 6–8.

Ingredients	*Utensils*
Butter	Flour sifter
Sugar	Mixing bowl
Rye flour	Measuring cup
All-purpose flour	Rolling pin
	Thimble
	Cookie sheet
	Spatula

RECIPE

Standard	*Metric*
1 cup butter	240 grams
2/3 cup sugar	160 grams
1 cup sifted rye flour	150 grams
1 1/4 cups sifted all-purpose flour	160 grams

METHOD

Cream butter and sugar until fluffy. Add rye flour and mix. Add all-purpose flour. Blend well. Chill. Take small amount of dough from the refrigerator and knead lightly. Roll out as thin as possible on floured counter.

Cut rounds about 2 1/2 inches in diameter. Cut center of cookies with a thimble; prick cookies with a fork. Place on buttered cookie sheets with a spatula or pancake turner. Repeat with the rest of the dough.

Bake 8–10 minutes in 350° F (177° C) oven. Let cool on cookie sheets.

Yield: 50 cookies.

13

Koek and Pannekoeken

There is a small country in Europe where a large part of the land has been made by its people. They have been exceedingly clever about the way they have done it and the use they have made of it. They have learned to manage it by centuries of back-breaking toil, a relentless fight with the sea, and the most intensive and scientific farming of any country in the world.

It all started thousands of years ago. Archeologists know that people were living in parts of the Netherlands at least 12,000 years ago. Then between 6000 and 4000 B.C. several Germanic tribes chose to live in these soggy parts that border the North Sea. If there were no natural heights to protect them from the incoming tides, they built their own mounds, called *terpen*, and built their homes, farmhouses, even villages upon them. In the summer they grew a bit of grain at the feet of the mounds, but hurried up the hill in the winter when the tides rose to drown their fields. They gradually increased the size of their *terpen* by heaping more rubbish and dirt around them and had a little more land for grain and cattle. They built sand dikes around the fields, but they were continually washed away. Then the Romans came and conquered them and taught them about other foods—cabbages, lentils, and plum trees. Most important of all, the road-building Romans built dikes along the swollen rivers to keep the roads high and dry. New pastures, yielding rich crops, appeared at the base of the dikes.

Finally the Romans left, but the river dikes, the new vegetables, and plum trees were there to stay. The centuries passed, more mounds were built in an area that was becoming rapidly crowded and more fields nestled against the mounds. But the powerful North Sea, the "Waterwolf," sought to prove its mastery. Around 1250 A.D. it broke through the dikes and sand dunes and changed the map of Holland. Instead of homes and fields, there were 1,000,000 acres of water in the middle of the Netherlands; a new sea, the Zuider Zee, was born.

Although the people cried, "What are we to do?" it was not long before they were doing something about it. They started to reclaim the land, and have been doing it successfully ever since, in spite of storms and floods. They first drained small lakes, using wind-driven mills to lift buckets of water out of the lake over and beyond newly built dikes of earth, and planted them to hold the earth together. They built a system of canals that emptied the water into the sea. Within the last 500 years half a million acres have been added to the Netherlands, and they are continually draining new areas with modern motor-driven pumps.

Beginning in 1920, they began to reclaim the Zuider Zee. They built a dike 100 yards wide and 20 miles long to close off the sea from the North Sea. Their plan, to reclaim five large *polders* (low land taken from the sea), will be completed in 1980. This will be an area of 850 square miles. Four of the polders have been completed and they have commenced work on the last. But the pumps must never be allowed to stop, day or night. As a taxi driver who lives north of Amsterdam told us, the water level would reach the third story of his home within one week if there should not be enough oil to keep the pumps running.

Every speck of land, natural or man made, must be used with the utmost care in this densely populated country. As long ago as 1750, the Dutch and their Flemish neighbors in Belgium were using organic fertilizers and a crop rotation sys-

tem to keep the land from losing its fertility. When the rest of Europe watched and learned from them, they adopted a four-crop rotation system that proved effective for them. Wheat was followed by turnips, the tops of which help smother weeds, barley was planted next, and then clover to enrich the soil.

European farming made notable gains in the eighteenth century. Even so, food was scarce and the cities were crowded. It is indeed fortunate that the development of grain in the New World began at this time. The Dutch grew large amounts of wheat in their colonial settlements along the Hudson River in the United States and in the southern part of Africa.

Today only one out of every ten people are farmers in the Netherlands. One-third of the fields are devoted to the cultivation of crops, the most important being wheat, rye, barley, oats, potatoes, and sugar beets. Most of the crops are raised for the seed that is exported to other countries. Consequently, the farmers are scientific agriculturalists; they attend special schools to learn the latest methods and the government is constantly helping them to improve.

Polder land, as is all of the farm land in the Netherlands, is in great demand. There are 300–400 applicants for every farm leased by the government. A farmer may lease the land for 12 years; if he manages it well, he may lease the land for another 12. Even an area adjacent to the runway at Schiphol Airport in Amsterdam is leased to men who harvest wheat.

It takes two to three years to prepare the polders for crops. First, huge ditches are dug on the new marshy soil, pipes are laid for drainage, roads are built, trees planted, and villages appear. A special plant called *coltsfoot*, a medicinal plant, is put into the soil, followed with reeds to absorb the remaining water. The field is then plowed. Sometimes parts of old ships are unearthed by the farmers' heavy mechanized plows. Linseed and winter rye are then planted, next lucerne, a kind of

Pumping station in a 56-mile-long dyke erected to drain waters from the Eastern Flevoland polder, in the Zuider Zee (Netherlands). *United Nations.*

North East Polder, Zuider Zee, Netherlands—an automatic potato extracting and sacking machine. *United Nations.*

alfalfa, and finally wheat and barley wave in a field of grain where storms once tossed the ships.

Cool misty weather and hard work contribute to huge appetites. The Dutch are fond of nourishing food made from the best ingredients. Although their grain yield is high per acre, they must import large quantities to satisfy their fondness for bread and cereals.

A Dutch breakfast is large. Basketfuls of bread, soft and white, and dark rye, are served with plates of thinly sliced Edam or Gouda cheese (their leading exports). Plenty of butter, jam, tea, coffee, or Dutch chocolate, and sometimes a soft-boiled egg accompany the bread. Children are often served a dish of cereal in addition.

The northernmost Dutch province of Friesland is a dairy industry center, with numerous cooperative dairies and many dairy products, including Edam and Gouda cheese, butter, milkpowder, condensed milk and casein. *United Nations.*

At eleven they treat themselves to more bread and coffee or cocoa, or a special buttered cake called a *koek*. From the Dutch word *koekje* (little cakes) the Americans made the word *cookie*.

Lunch is another bread and butter meal. Sometimes the children have a special treat of "chocolate bread"—bread and butter with chocolate shavings sprinkled on it. Prepared meats or thin slices of ham may be served with the cheese at lunchtime.

Four o'clock is teatime with cakes, cookies, or chocolates for special occasions. Six o'clock is dinnertime, the first hot meal, unless it is served at midday as in some parts of the Netherlands. Then dinner is a bread and butter meal. Dinner mainly consists of a hot soup, meat or fish and potatoes, and sometimes fruit to finish. Often huge dinner-plate-sized *pannekoeken* with sliced apples or bacon in the batter are served for dessert. They are served hot with sugar, butter, molasses, or whipped cream. Pancakes (made with yeast) have always been a Dutch favorite.

KOEK / A Dutch Breakfast Cake

Ingredients	Utensils
Brown sugar	Loaf pan
Honey	Large mixing bowl
Egg	Measuring spoons and cups
Molasses (dark)	Cooling rack
Baking soda	
Baking powder	
Butter	
Salt	
Allspice, nutmeg, cinnamon, ginger	
All-purpose flour	
Rye flour	

RECIPE

Standard	Metric
1/2 cup dark brown sugar	125 grams

1 egg
1/2 cup honey   135 ml
3 tablespoons dark molasses   45 ml
1 teaspoon baking soda   5 grams
1/2 teaspoon baking powder   3 grams
1/3 teaspoon each, salt,
   allspice, nutmeg, cinnamon,
   ginger   2 grams
2 tablespoons melted butter   30 ml
3/4 cup all-purpose flour   105 grams
3/4 cup rye flour   112 grams

METHOD

Beat egg, sugar, and salt in large mixing bowl. Add honey and
molasses, soda, baking powder, melted butter, and spices. Mix
well. Gradually add all-purpose and rye flour sifted together.

Grease loaf pan. Fill 2/3 full with cake batter. Bake in preheated oven at 350° F (177° C) for 45–50 minutes. Cool in pan 5
minutes then empty on rack.

GROENTESOEP / Dutch Vegetable Soup with Barley

Ingredients	Utensils
Leeks	Sauce pan, large
Celery root	Colander
Carrots	Measuring cup or metric
Green beans	container
Peas	sauce pan for cooking barley
Celery	
Salt and pepper	
Barley, cooked	
Butter	
Chopped parsley or celery greens	
Soup stock	

Standard	Metric
2 leeks	
1/2 cup each sliced carrots, peas, green beans, celery	125 grams
6 cups stock or	1440 ml
4 (10 3/4 oz) cans bouillon	305 grams
3 tablespoons butter	45 grams
1 tablespoon each of chopped parsley and celery greens	15 grams
1/2 cup barley	100 grams
cooked in	
1 cup water	250 ml

METHOD

Wash vegetables. Cut into small uniform pieces. Wash and strain in colander.

Place butter in large sauce pan. Sauté vegetables in bottom of pan for 2 minutes. Add soup stock or bouillon. Simmer 10 minutes until vegetables are barely done and crisp. Season. Add chopped parsley and celery greens. Add cooked barley. Serve at once.

Serves 6.

OLIEBOLLEN

A traditional New Year's Eve treat in Holland, similar to doughnuts, they are fried in deep fat in a skillet and eaten warm, dusted with powdered sugar.

Ingredients	Utensils
Yeast	Skillet
Milk	Measuring cups, liquid and
Flour	dry, and measuring spoons
Egg	Teaspoon

Raisins
1 apple
Shortening for deep frying

Flour sifter
Bowl
Sauce pan
Tongs
Wooden spoon

RECIPE

Standard	*Metric*
1 package dry yeast	7 grams
1 cup warm milk	240 ml
2 1/3 cups flour, sifted	300 grams
1 egg	
1 cup raisins	200 grams
1 apple sliced and chopped	100 grams
1–2 cups shortening for deep frying	226–452 grams

METHOD

Warm milk in sauce pan. Slice apples and cut into small pieces. Sift flour and measure.

In a bowl blend the yeast with a little of the warm milk. After 5 minutes add the rest of the milk, the sifted and measured flour, egg, raisins, and apple. Stir well. Set aside in a warm place until the batter has doubled in size.

Form the batter into small pieces with a teaspoon. Fry for 8 minutes in skillet with enough hot shortening to reach height of 1 1/2 inches. Drain on a paper towel after removing each oliebollen with tongs. Sprinkle with powdered sugar and serve.

Serves 8.

NEVER leave the skillet when deep frying. Have a package of soda or a lid nearby to smother any grease flame that might occur from fat that becomes too hot.

❧WATERGRUEL / A Famous Old Dutch Cereal

Ingredients	*Utensils*
Barley flakes (health food stores)	Measuring cups or metric container
Sugar	Sauce pan
Cranberry juice	Wooden spoon
Raisins	
Lemon peel	
Stick cinnamon	

RECIPE

Standard	*Metric*
3 cups water	720 ml
3/4 cup sugar	180 grams
1 cup barley flakes	100 grams
1 cup cranberry juice	240 ml
1/2 cup raisins	180 grams
Piece of lemon peel	
Stick of cinnamon	

METHOD

Cook the barley flakes in the water with cinnamon stick and lemon peel for 10 minutes. Add cranberry juice, raisins, and sugar, and cook 5 minutes more.

Take out lemon peel and cinnamon before serving.

❧PANNEKOEKAN / Dutch Pancakes

These pancakes are as large as a dinner plate or even larger. They are served either with smoked sausage or bacon, or as a dessert with molasses or golden syrup and butter.

Ingredients	*Utensils*
Yeast	Bowl for mixing
All-purpose flour	Measuring cups or metric container
Salt	Skillet, large
Butter	
Molasses or syrup	

RECIPE

Standard	Metric
1 package dry yeast	7 grams
1/4 cup warm water	60 ml
4 cups all-purpose flour	560 grams
1 teaspoon salt	5 grams
4 cups lukewarm milk	960 ml

METHOD

Dissolve yeast in 1/4 cup warm water. Sift flour and salt. Add half the milk to the yeast solution and mix. Add remaining milk slowly. Let stand in warm place for 1 hour.

Preheat skillet, melt 1 tablespoon (15 grams) butter in skillet. Add enough batter to cover bottom of skillet. Brown lightly on one side then turn and brown other side. Serve hot.

Yield: 4–5 large pancakes.

🌿 WAFFLES

A Dutch favorite that may be served at any meal. A bride in Holland receives her own waffle iron with her initials engraved on it. Many are beautifully decorated. Some Dutch brides brought their long-handled waffle irons to New Amsterdam (New York City) to bake fine waffles in the hearths of their homes in the New World.

Ingredients	Utensils
Barley flour	Waffle iron
All-purpose flour	Wooden spoon
Baking powder (double-acting)	Flour sifter
Salt	Measuring cups, dry and
Sugar	liquid, and measuring
Butter	spoons
Milk	Sauce pan
Eggs	2 bowls

199

RECIPE

Standard	Metric
1/2 cup barley flour	60 grams
1 cup all-purpose flour	140 grams
2 teaspoons double-acting baking powder	10 grams
2 eggs, well beaten	
2 cups milk	480 ml
2 teaspoons sugar	10 grams
1/3 cup melted butter	80 ml
1 teaspoon salt	5 grams

METHOD

Sift flour and measure. Resift into a large bowl with sugar, salt, and baking powder. Melt butter in a sauce pan. Pour butter and milk into the flour mixture. Mix with a wooden spoon.

Beat eggs with a rotary beater in another bowl. Add eggs to batter. Beat out any lumps in the batter with wooden spoon.

Preheat waffle iron. A signal light will go off when the iron is ready. Pour in just enough batter to make a full waffle. Close lid. Do not open until waffle stops steaming, about 2–3 minutes. Remove waffle with a fork and serve hot.

Let the waffle iron remain open until you bake the next waffle.

Serve with syrup, whipped cream, chocolate sauce, or jam.

Serves 6.

❧14❧
Groundnut Stew and Ugali

A new emphasis is being placed upon an old, old grain by people in the United States who maintain that millet is the only grain that contains all of the vitamins and minerals that are needed for good nutrition. Grain sorghum, a type of millet, was brought to South Carolina from Africa in 1700 as food for the slaves. Long used as food by the northern Chinese, who give it credit for their increase in stature over that of their southern countrymen, its cultivation has been rapidly increased throughout the United States since World War II, but mainly for animal feed.

Millet contains more protein than corn. Its stems and leaves resemble those of corn, but the grains grow in clusters at the top of the stem, rather than in ears of grain. The plant will thrive on a small amount of water, but does need a warm climate. It is a sturdy plant, sometimes growing to a height of fifteen feet.

The ancient Egyptians cultivated millet as a cereal at least 4200 years ago. Later the Romans used it to make the grain porridge called *puls.* But evidence now shows that it was first cultivated by people who lived along the Niger River, south of the Sahara Desert, in an area that now comprises parts of Senegal, Guinea, Mali, and Gambia. Archeologists are discovering that there were wealthy and culturally advanced empires

Three types of millet from *History of Mankind* by Freidrich Ratzel. Macmillan, New York, 1896–98.   *New York Public Library, Picture Collection.*

in ancient Africa. As they traded with one another, the cultivation of millet slowly spread throughout the continent except in the small rain-forest area.

Some Africans were cattle herders, a few food gatherers, but most were and are farmers. Then as now, the men clear the fields by burning the brush to provide minerals and fertilizers for the generally poor topsoil. Traditionally it has been the women's responsibility to plant the grain, to harvest, and to crush it into meal in a large mortar and pestle. They do not plow the fields; instead they use a hoe or a digging stick. A plowed field would lose a great deal of the precious topsoil at the first rain. Crops of peanuts (called groundnuts), squash, and sesame seeds border the fields.

A young African country girl is taught her first lessons in cookery when she is five or six years old. She helps her mother select the greens and firewood necessary for the preparation of the evening meal. In a special hut, a fire is built within stones that are set in a triangular pattern. An iron pot is placed over the fire. Grain that has been pounded into a paste is placed in boiling water and cooked into a thick porridge. In another pot a stew composed of a little meat, vegetables, and a strong red pepper seasoning is simmered. The porridge is served from a common bowl at mealtime. Each person care-

Women harvesting rice in Senegal. An improved variety has been introduced here, giving larger yields.   *United Nations/Photo by Ray Witlin.*

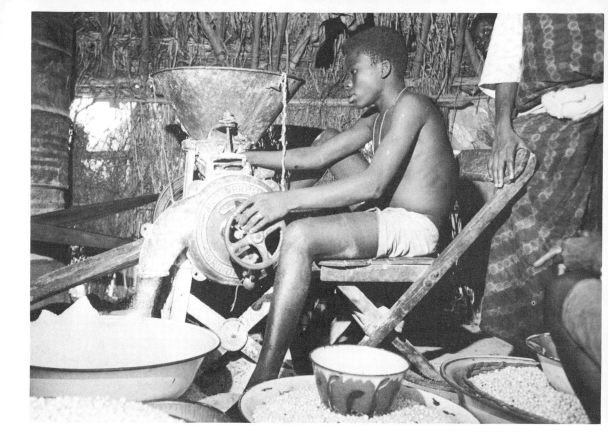

A ten-year-old Dahomean boy grinding maize.   *United Nations.*

fully selects a morsel, using only three fingers of his right hand. He then deftly rolls it into an oval ball and makes a depression in it with his thumb. The grain serves as a spoon that is dipped into the hot stew that has been placed into individual wooden bowls. Sometimes a kind of bread made of corn or millet flour is baked in the ashes of the fire. The African slaves in America made it and called it hoe cake or ash cake.

In fact, much of our southern cuisine reflects the African influence. The women proved to be excellent cooks in the plantation kitchens, and they cooked in the slave compounds as they had in Africa. They brought sorghum to the United States along with okra, black-eyed peas, peanuts, and sesame seeds, called benne seeds by the southerners. They hunted in the fields and woods to supplement the grain sorghum or corn-meal. Another kind of sorghum, a sweet variety, was used for syrup by boiling the stems and obtaining the residue that is often used instead of molasses.

Whenever women get together, they like to trade recipes. So it was in the southern slave compounds. Women from different parts of Africa, east, west, and central, were grouped together for the first time. An international African cuisine developed in America.

A proof of the nutritional value of African millet or grain sorghum (called guinea corn in the West Indies) is the fact that the captured Africans who best endured the long and horrible voyage to the West Indies and the United States were the farmers who were used to eating large amounts of whole grain

Conakry, Guinea. A study in contrast: modern buildings and old shacks.
United Nations.

in Africa. The agricultural tribes were in the greatest demand at the slave markets because they were the healthiest.

In spite of the unfortunate slave trade, the world of the eighteenth century remained in ignorance of the culture and artistic and musical ability of the African people. Even the Portuguese, Dutch, and other European explorers who came to the continent to buy gold, ivory, spices, and eventually people from the African kings, only touched upon its shores and kept secret what they had learned from the rest of the world. Even when the slave trade ended, Europe began a period of colonial rule in Africa that was more of a benefit to themselves than to the people of Africa. European culture, language, and cuisine were imposed upon those who lived in the cities. However, beautiful cities were built, educational centers developed, and transportation facilities were introduced by the colonists.

Beginning in the 1960s, Africa, still a mystery to most of the world, became a birthplace of several new nations that declared their independence from colonial rule, just as the United States had done in 1776.

New nations have many problems and many lessons to learn. African nations are beginning to realize that their most important task is to develop better agriculture for themselves rather than turn all of their attention to industry and cities. They are also learning that a devotion to cash crops such as coffee, cocoa, peanuts, and rubber does not meet the demand of the people for more and better food. The farmers need to be taught new methods of agriculture, of irrigation, fertilization, and pest control, so that they may get higher yields in spite of poor soil and little rainfall.

A national cuisine is developing in the growing middle class of Africa that reflects the traditional ways of cooking together with some European refinements. Meals are served on attractive cloths, beautifully designed following old traditional patterns in local cotton mills. Carved wooden bowls hold fruits that accompany the seasoned main dishes and fufu or ugali, as the grain porridges are called. Women still prefer to cook outdoors in a courtyard just outside of their homes. Hibachis or charcoal braziers are used in the home economics classes. Colorful open markets with an abundance of fresh fruits and vegetables and spices of the area are visited each day by the housewives, but they also enjoy the benefits of the supermarkets with their packaged seasonings, prepared peanut butter, and ready ground flour—even canned or frozen foods. Restaurants and hotels now offer representative African dinners with foods that are fresh and combined in interesting ways. What follows is a sampling of the way Africans use millet grain in their everyday cooking.

Primitive plowing methods still used by some Ethiopian farmers.

United Nations.

Millet is becoming increasingly popular because of its nutritional value. It may be purchased at health food stores. Some supermarkets carry it if they have a specialty food department. A light tangy cereal may be made from the following recipe:

Ingredients	Utensils
Whole grain millet	Measuring cups and spoons
Cottage cheese	Large sauce pan
Milk	Wooden spoon
Honey	Serving bowl

RECIPE

Standard	Metric
1 cup millet	200 grams
2 cups water	480 ml
1 cup cottage cheese	240 grams
1/2 cup milk	120 ml

METHOD

Place water in sauce pan and bring to a boil. Add millet and cook for 5 minutes. Reduce heat and simmer until most of the liquid evaporates, about 20 minutes. Place in serving bowl, add cottage cheese, and stir. Place in cereal bowls, sweeten with honey (about 1 teaspoon per person), add milk from milk pitcher, and enjoy a hot cereal.

Serves 4.

✣WEST AFRICAN GROUNDNUT STEW
served with a Ugali of millet meal and whole grain millet

Ingredients	Utensils
Stewing beef (2–3 lb chicken may be used, boned and cut into small pieces)	Skillet
	Large sauce pan
	Measuring spoons and cups
Onion	Wooden spoon

Garlic
Ginger root
Peanut oil
Peanut butter
Canned tomatoes
Frozen okra
Hardboiled eggs
Cayenne pepper
Black pepper
Salt

Knife
Large bowl

RECIPE

Standard	Metric
1 lb stewing beef or chicken	500 grams
1 large onion, sliced	140 grams
1 clove garlic, sliced	10 grams
1/4″ ginger root, sliced	
1/4 cup peanut oil	60 ml
1/4 cup peanut butter	75 grams
1 (16 oz) can tomatoes	450 grams
1 pkg (16 oz) frozen okra	283 grams
3 hardboiled eggs	
1/2–1 teaspoon cayenne pepper	5 grams
1/2 teaspoon black pepper	3 grams
1/2 teaspoon salt	3 grams

METHOD

Place 1/4 cup peanut oil in a large skillet. When it is hot, add the sliced garlic clove and ginger. Add sliced onions and cook until they are brown. Remove to large sauce pan.

In the same skillet and oil quickly fry the meat that has been cut into 1 inch cubes. Remove to sauce pan with the onions. Add 1 can tomatoes, can of water (same size as tomatoes), peanut butter, and seasonings, and bring to a boil. Add this mixture to stew.

Reduce heat and simmer uncovered for 45 minutes to 1 hour. Add frozen okra and sliced hardboiled egg. Cook 10 more minutes.

209

Serve in large bowl accompanied with bowls of any of the following: Ugali (recipe follows), sliced pineapple, sliced cucumbers, sliced bananas sprinkled with lemon juice, shredded coconut, unsalted peanuts, boiled rice, sliced papayas (if available), watermelon balls (if available), canned yams, heated. In Africa yams or grains such as rice and corn are mashed into balls called FuFu.

Serves 2.

UGALI-MILLET

Ingredients	Utensils
Millet meal	Wooden spoon
Whole grain millet	Sauce pan
Water	Measuring cup and spoons
	Skillet for Maasa

RECIPE

Standard	Metric
1 1/2 cups cooked whole grain millet	300 grams
1/2 cup millet meal	75 grams
1 1/2 cups water	360 ml

METHOD

Mix cooked millet and millet meal in a bowl. [For 1 1/2 cups cooked millet, cook 1 cup millet (200 grams) in 2 cups boiling water (480 ml) for 5 minutes. Reduce heat and simmer 20 minutes.]

Place water in sauce pan and bring to boil. Add mixed millet meal and whole grain millet mixture. Cook until the Ugali is a very thick porridge. Stir constantly with wooden spoon.

Traditionally the Ugali is served with the stew in another bowl. A ball of it is gathered and dipped into the stew. It may be made into spoon-sized dumplings dropped into stew, or it may be sliced into 1/2-inch-thick slices. The slices may be fried in small amount of peanut oil in a skillet. It is then called Maasa. Place slices on plate and spoon stew over the Maasa.

Serves 4–6.

❧COCONUT MILLET PUDDING

Ingredients   *Utensils*
Shredded coconut   Double boiler
Millet meal   Measuring spoons and
Milk   cups
Sugar   Wooden spoon
Vanilla   6 custard dishes
Salt
Chocolate syrup or fruit
  preserve

RECIPE

Standard	Metric
2 cups milk, scalded	480 ml
1/2 cup sugar	120 grams
1/4 cup millet meal	40 grams
1 cup shredded coconut	80 grams
1 teaspoon vanilla extract	5 ml
6 teaspoons chocolate syrup or	85 ml
6 teaspoons fruit jam or preserves	50 grams
1 teaspoon salt	5 grams

METHOD

Place milk that has been scalded in top part of double boiler. Add sugar, millet meal, and place over bottom of double boiler that is 1/3 full of boiling water. Cook for 15 minutes stirring occasionally. Add coconut and salt. Stir and cook 10 more minutes. Add vanilla. Pour into custard cups and chill. Place one teaspoon of chocolate syrup in center of each custard before serving (if fruit preserve is preferred, follow same procedure). Serve as dessert.

Serves 6.

❧15❧
Cornbread and Tamale Pie

If someone could build a railroad track clear around the equator, and place upon it a train that could carry all of the corn that was cultivated last year in the United States, there would not be room left on the tracks for the train to go anyplace. Although each American consumes, on the average, sixty-four pounds of corn a year, ninety percent of the crop will be fed to livestock. The stalks, leaves, and cobs that are left are used industrially to make all kinds of products—paper, cardboard, wallboards, pastes, adhesives, etc. No wonder more acres are planted in corn than any other crop, and next year's crop should yield six billion bushels. We also cultivate huge amounts of wheat, enough for ourselves and for many areas in Europe, Asia, and Africa.

When Christopher Columbus and his companions saw corn growing in the New World, they called it *maize* and took some back to Europe. Every explorer who came to this continent reported on its cultivation by the Indians that they encountered. It is believed that the first settlers in America, the Indians, came from Asia when there was a land bridge to Alaska. They came in two migrations shortly after the end of the last ice age. Upon arriving, they gradually spread out over the two Americas. Scientists have felt sure of this fact for some time, but the basic food of the Indians, corn, was a mystery until the last decade.

Aztec corn. From *Big Book of Indians* by Sydney E. Fletcher. Grosset & Dunlap, 1950. *New York Public Library, Picture Collection.*

It was a mystery that tantalized them for years. Even Charles Darwin and Luther Burbank could not find the answer. Because no evidence could be found anywhere of wild corn that could reseed itself and grow without human aid, the question remained: How and where did it begin? The Indians called it the gift of the gods.

A tiny ear of a kind of popcorn was found in Bat Cave in New Mexico. It was carbon dated to be 6000 years old. Someone must have planted it since the cob was not constructed so that the kernels or seeds could detach themselves to grow new plants. Finally, the mystery was solved. Archeologists searching for the answer were rewarded when they examined thirty-nine caves south of Mexico City. The area seemed favorable. Ancient spores of corn had been discovered deep in the ground near Mexico City. In the thirty-ninth cave, they found tiny little ears of corn about one-half inch in length. Each hard kernel on the ear was separately wrapped in its own husk instead of a single husk covering the whole ear. Furthermore,

213

An Indian village of the Manhattans prior to the occupation of the Dutch from *Valentine's Manual*, 1858.   *Museum of the City of New York.*

the kernels were easily dislodged and could scatter on the ground to grow new plants. Together with the beans and squash remains found in the cave, the corn was ascertained to be about 7500 years old. It is now thought that new crops cultivated by the Indians gradually choked out the parent plant, but from it six different varieties were developed before the settlers arrived from Europe.

If there had not been Indians living near the Northeast coast when the English arrived in Plymouth, the new colony would have starved, as the seeds of wheat that they had brought with them had partially rotted and the remainder did not thrive in the rocky soil of New England. Luckily they learned to plant corn, Indian fashion. First, six or seven kernels were placed in mounds, then as soon as the corn plants were a few inches high, beans were planted around them to climb the stalks, then squash and pumpkins trailed their vines over the ground at the feet of the stalks. The Indians also taught them the benefits of turkeys as food, and showed them how to gather clams on the shores, but they were indeed thankful when they finally had grain to pound into meal to make hasty pudding or johnnycake. No wonder they were happy to share their Thanksgiving feast with their tutors.

Over the fireplaces of their crudely built houses, kettles of corn and beans (succotash), clams, and pumpkins finally hung from a green pole placed directly over the flames. When iron was discovered in 1642, cranes replaced the breakable poles and each housewife possessed two iron kettles which she kept in constant use, while her husband shared an iron plow with his neighbor.

The Dutch who settled in the fertile regions of New York were prosperous at once. They erected windmills to grind their bountiful harvests of wheat and corn. Within a short time coffee cakes and sweet cakes, cruellers and oliebollen (Dutch doughnuts) were sold at public bakeries. Each housewife made her waffles on the long-handled waffle iron that she had carefully brought from Holland, while her children happily tasted the koekies that were used to test the heat of the ovens for the baking of larger cakes.

William Penn, the founder of Pennsylvania, had circulated pamphlets advertising his colony in Holland, England, and Germany. The Germans and Dutch who were attracted to the settlements had been practicing scientific agriculture (crop rotation and fertilizing) in Europe, and they brought that skill with them to the New World. Consequently, Pennsylvania and the other Mid-Atlantic colonies began in 1754 to ship large amounts of wheat and flour to England and southern Europe, and to the northern and southern colonies in America. The Mid-Atlantic states remained the "breadbasket" until the early nineteenth century.

The soil was too rich and the climate too warm for wheat in the South, although corn grew well enough as it does in every

Threshing and cleaning grain. U.S. Patent Office. *The Growth of Industrial Art*. Benjamin Butterworth, Commissioner of Patents. Washington: Government Printing Office, 1892.   *New York Public Library, Picture Collection.*

216

state on the continent. Cornbread was and is a favorite, but beaten biscuits made with wheat flour were a special treat. For one-half hour the dough was beaten on a hard board in order to bring some air into the mixture to make the biscuits rise. Baking powder eased the task a great deal when it was introduced in 1856.

Another grain, rice, was introduced in Charleston, South Carolina, when a ship returning from Madagascar sought refuge from a storm in Charleston Harbor. The captain of the ship gave Dr. Henry Woodward a thank you gift of a bag of rice from Madagascar in return for the hospitality that Dr. Woodward had offered. The doctor planted some of the rice seeds, gave some to friends who in turn found that the grain grew exceedingly well in the swampy land that surrounds the city. Charleston became one of the richest cities in the South, as well as one of the loveliest in America. It was also an important port city. Many plantation owners built second homes, townhouses with wide verandas facing Charleston Harbor, to give their families a relief from the heat of the country. Some of the plantations still remain along the Ashley River and some, such as the Middleton Plantation, have been opened to the public. Although the main part of the Middleton house was destroyed during the Civil War, a large wing remains. The view across the gardens to the river reveals a picturesque rice mill, square ponds for the cultivation of the crop that needs to stand in water, the dock where the bags of rice were loaded onto waiting ships, some ancient oak trees with moss trailing from their branches, and one of the most exquisite camellia gardens imaginable.

All of the cooking was done in fireplaces that were built separate from the plantation or townhouse. The black women who ruled their domain in the kitchen were well prepared to cook in a hot climate.

Grain sorghum was first brought to South Carolina in 1700 as food for the slaves. The seeds were ground into a meal used in the manner of cornmeal for flour, pancakes, mush, and puddings. It requires longer cooking than cornmeal. Grain sorghum is more nutritious than corn but is grown today for stock feed rather than human consumption. The stalks of sweet sorghum are ground or crushed to make a sweet syrup that may replace molasses in a recipe.

The slaves brought new and interesting methods of seasoning from West Africa and exerted a strong influence on southern cuisine. As previously mentioned, grain sorghum, okra, black-eyed peas, sesame seeds (called benne seeds in South Carolina), and peanuts were added to southern gardens.

Ninety percent of the people were engaged in farming in 1790, and the majority of them possessed small farms where they grew all that they needed. In addition to the fifty to sixty man-hours that were spent on a single acre of wheat, farmers had to do their own carpentry work, slaughter their livestock, and make their tools. The women were the bread-makers, the butter-churners, the cloth-weavers, and the dressmakers. Cloth was woven from home-grown flax or from the wool of sheep. They had few hours for fun and relaxation.

Very few of them were scientific farmers. They used wasteful methods on the soil, although Benjamin Franklin, Thomas Jefferson, and George Washington were intensely interested in using the soil advantageously. George Washington, an excellent farmer himself, was proud of the wheat cultivated and ground in his mill at Mt. Vernon.

The Northwest Ordinance of 1787 encouraged a rapid settlement of lands beyond the Allegheny Mountains. Once more forests had to be cleared so that the corn and wheat could be planted on new and fertile soil. Settlers from Germany, Holland, England, and the Scandinavian countries joined the Americans who had left their homelands near the Atlantic Ocean.

There was more than enough land for every newcomer. As Thomas Jefferson said, "In Europe, the object is to make the

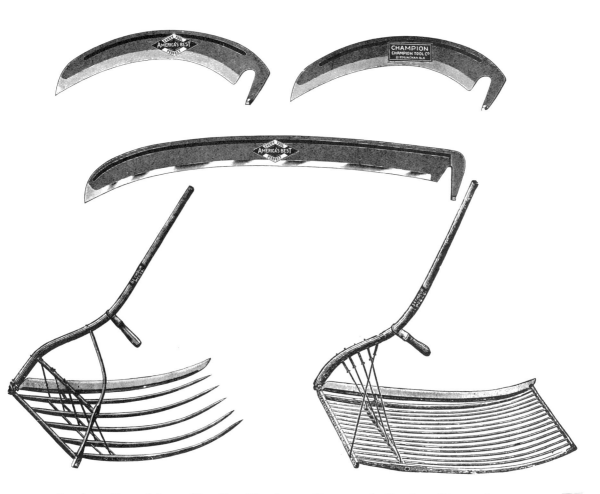

Scythes. From Moore-Handley Hardware Company's Catalog. Birmingham, Alabama, before 1918. *New York Public Library, Picture Collection.*

most of the land, labor being abundant; here, it is to make the most of our labor, land being abundant." It was undoubtedly the shortage of labor that necessitated the invention of machinery to lighten the load of each farmer. Plows were manufactured of sturdy steel in 1825. The McCormick Reaper was invented in 1830. Next came a mechanical thresher and a twine binder. Now, huge combines cut, thresh, clean, sack, and weigh the grain.

The Homestead Act of 1862 encouraged the hardy and adventurous to take their plows and possessions ever farther

The Rocky Mountains, emigrants crossing the plains. Currier & Ives, 1866.
Museum of the City of New York.

west into the Great Plains. A head of a family was given 160 acres of land if he lived on it and farmed it for five years. Windmills were turning on the treeless plains to pump up water to irrigate new crops. Houses were built of sod as wood was scarce. Barbed wire fences were placed around farms to discourage the marauding cattle rustlers who resented the new homesteaders. It was a repetition of the events that had occurred centuries before upon the plains of Eastern Europe.

Some of the new settlers came from Eastern Europe. They brought seeds with them from the Russian Ukraine, the wheat belt of Europe, which were well suited to the climate of the Northern Plains. Not all of the seeds from Europe produced good crops, but experimentation led to the garnering of those best suited to the new land.

220

Benjamin Franklin and Thomas Jefferson were the first to exchange seeds with other American growers. Franklin brought rhubarb from Scotland while Jefferson, you may recall, risked the death penalty when he smuggled rice seeds out of Italy. In 1817, Elkanay Watson of New York sent a letter to various consuls in Europe requesting seeds. He received fourteen varieties of wheat, one variety of oats, and one of barley in a sealed cask. An enthusiastic botanist in Valencia, Spain, had selected types that he hoped would grow well in this country and dispatched them in this manner. Farmers in New York made a favorable report on one of the varieties.

The demand for seeds was heightened by the westward expansion. The United States government distributed more than eighty thousand packets each year. We received gifts of two important crops from Europe—sugar beets from France and Germany, durum wheat from Russia—and the navel orange from Brazil. Varieties of rice from the Orient were cultivated in the coastal plains of Louisiana and Texas.

Two other bills were passed in 1862 that were a benefit to the farmer. The Department of Agriculture was established by Abraham Lincoln, thereby ensuring a thorough study of plants, their resistance to disease, and the best methods of cultivation. Another bill proposed that federally owned land would be given to each state for a college to teach the branches of learning that were related to agriculture. Iowa was the first state to accept the provisions of the Land-Grant Act. One hundred boys and girls came together to take one of the two courses offered: agriculture or mechanics. Today, students are enrolled in colleges in five areas at Iowa State. They may choose agriculture, engineering, home economics, humanities, or veterinary medicine. Every state has a similar university.

I was a teenager when we moved from the Midwest to live in California. Driving through Iowa, Nebraska, and Kansas we saw nothing but miles and miles and miles of corn. Finally, the scene changed in Colorado; there were mountains in the

The Farmer's Home-Harvest. Currier & Ives, 1864. The Harry T. Peters
Collection.   *Museum of the City of New York.*

distance. But before we could get to them we passed by acres
of sugar beets growing in the fields. When we left the Rocky
Mountains, a magnificent spectacle to anyone who has lived on
flat lands for most of his life, we entered the Southwest. Here
Indians could be seen living in pueblos, the Spanish name for
village, grinding corn between stones as they have always
done and baking their corn bread in dome-shaped ovens built
out-of-doors.

When we arrived in California, I made new friends in high
school who spoke of *tamales* and *tacos* and *enchiladas* or *chili
con carne.* All were very strange names to me; I was used to
having stewed chicken and dumplings with strawberry short-
cake made with baking powder biscuits every Sunday, or beef

and vegetables and peanut butter sandwiches every single day. Even the avocados that grew so well on a tree in our new backyard were strange to me. I was not very adventurous, so it was some time before I tasted the new foods.

I learned that I had missed a great deal. Now the Spanish and Mexican food that is so much a part of the diet of the Southwest and West is regularly on my menu, as well as Italian, Hungarian, German, Chinese, and French foods. The West abounds in all types of cuisines because people from many countries have made their homes here. Truly the "melting pot" that is America must have begun in the kitchen when housewives exchanged recipes with their neighbors from other countries. American cooks like to experiment with new dishes although they retain and cherish the recipes that they received from their parents.

Long before the English landed on the eastern coast, Spanish missions were established in the Southwest and California. At first, rice, wheat, and vegetables were the only crops grown on the mission farms. Later groves of citrus fruits and vineyards were added.

Alaska was the last state to be farmed. Not until 1935 when the United States government transported 200 farm families to brave long, dark winters was anyone hardy enough to try to cultivate crops in a brief growing season in south-central Alaska. Their courage was rewarded with lush fields of wheat and other crops that are produced in the Matanuska Valley.

Although farming is the chief industry of Hawaii, three-fourths of the land is devoted to sugar cane, which is sent to California to be refined. Some rice is grown, but most of the island's food supply is sent from the mainland.

The greatest problem of the farmer of the twentieth century has been the cultivation of too much grain. It began during World War I when our allies depended upon us for their grain supplies. They regained their self-sufficiency after the war, while our farm surplus increased.

Again during World War II we supplied a war-wracked Europe with grain, and the problem of surpluses departed only to return again in 1953. Some of the surplus grain was given to schools for the school lunch program, while a great deal was given to countries in need. It has been a continuing aid program in which grain and other foods account for one-half of the total gift. Other nations in the New World that contribute from their surplus are the Dominion of Canada, Australia, Argentina, and Brazil. All of them have made tremendous growth in the cultivation of corn and wheat.

Recently some countries have demanded more and more grain because of poor crop harvests. Areas in India, Africa, and South America have been threatened with famine. Our surpluses disappeared, and our storage bins were emptied.

In 1973 Congress enacted the Agricultural and Consumer Act that is designed to increase production still further. Although we are the world's largest exporter of grain, we have made amazing advances in the technology of agriculture, and we are growing better crops than at any time in the past.

However, there are limits to the amount of aid that any one country can give. Many nations under the auspices of the United Nations are beginning to realize that famine and starvation are world problems. Consequently, they are regularly donating additional amounts of grain.

In 1974, a World Food Council, consisting of representatives from thirty-six countries, was set up. The Council endorsed the establishment of a cereal reserve, a commitment of at least 10 million tons of cereal per year to the nations in need, and the strengthening of their agricultural programs, including research and technical assistance. For the first time in history, most of the nations of the world are concerned with the well-being of the citizens of other countries.

Recipes as well as food are being shared. It is always interesting to taste the specialties of a neighbor, near or far, and to learn how to make them. As we have noted, the American kitchen has become a true "melting pot" flavored by the foods of its many citizens from the Old World. Yet we have some dishes that were developed within the United States and that are a part of our national heritage and history.

One example is Yankee Corn Bread, or Corn Pone, originally made from meal ground at the village water mill.

YANKEE CORN BREAD

In the early days, johnnycake (journey cake) as it was called in New England, or corn pone, ash cake, or hoecake, in the South, was made of cornmeal, water, and salt mixed into a stiff dough and baked on a warm hearth or a hoe placed over an open fire in the fields. Ash cakes kept many a Confederate soldier alive during the Civil War. This is a more modern version of corn pone.

Ingredients	*Utensils*
Yellow cornmeal	Large bowl
All-purpose flour	Sauce pan
Baking powder	Electric mixer or wooden
Eggs	spoon
Melted butter or margarine	Measuring cup and spoons
Milk	Square cake pan (9"x 9")

RECIPE

Standard	*Metric*
1 1/2 cups yellow cornmeal	225 grams
3/4 cup all-purpose flour	105 grams
1 tablespoon baking powder	15 grams
2 eggs well beaten	
1/4 cup melted margarine	60 grams
1 cup buttermilk and 1 teaspoon soda or 1 cup milk	240 ml, 5 grams
1 teaspoon salt	5 grams

METHOD

In a large bowl mix the cornmeal, all-purpose flour, baking powder, soda, salt. Beat eggs, add with milk and shortening all at once. (Melt shortening in sauce pan). Stir slightly until flour is simply moist. DO NOT STIR TOO MUCH.

Bake in a 9 x 9 greased pan for 20 minutes at 400° F (205° C). Cut into squares and serve warm with butter.

Serves 8.

AWENDAW / Baked Hominy

Hominy is a favorite in the Carolinas. It is a corn preparation that was often served for breakfast and eaten with bacon or fish cakes, or baked according to this recipe and served in the evening. Boiled hominy was often sold in the streets of eastern cities.

Ingredients	*Utensils*
Hominy	Sauce pan
Butter	Rotary egg beater
Milk	Measuring container and
Cornmeal	spoons
Salt	Baking dish
Eggs	

RECIPE

Standard	*Metric*
1 can hominy (29 oz)	822 grams
1 1/2 tablespoons butter	20 grams
3 eggs	
1 1/2 cups milk	360 ml
1 cup cornmeal	200 grams
1/2 teaspoon salt	

METHOD

Heat hominy in sauce pan. While it is still hot, add butter and

226

beaten eggs. Gradually add milk. Add cornmeal and salt. The batter is like thick custard. Pour into 1-quart baking dish that has been greased. Bake at 375° F (191° C) for 35 minutes.

Serves 6–8.

SORGHUM MOLASSES RAISIN BREAD

Although molasses from the sugar cane was the prime sweetener in America until the close of the Civil War, it was often replaced by sorghum molasses in some areas of the South, especially in the Smoky and Ozark mountain areas. The syrup looks and tastes like molasses. The stalks of sorghum are ground and crushed and boiled to make the syrup that contains many vitamins and a great deal of iron.

Ingredients	*Utensils*
Milk	Mixing bowl
Shortening	Measuring containers and
Sorghum molasses or molasses	spoons
Raisins	Warm damp cloth
Salt	Mixing spoon or electric
Yeast	mixer
Flour	Two loaf pans

RECIPE

Standard	*Metric*
2 cups milk, scalded and warm	480 ml
2 tablespoons melted shortening	30 grams
1/4 cup sorghum molasses	60 ml
1 1/2 teaspoons salt	7 grams
1 cup raisins	200 grams
1 oz yeast	7 grams
5 1/2–6 cups flour, all-purpose or	
1/2 whole wheat, 1/2 all-purpose	840 grams

METHOD

Scald milk in sauce pan. Combine with melted shortening and molasses. Cool. Add yeast and allow to stand 5 minutes. Add raisins, then flour, a little at a time. Mix well. Knead on a floured counter for 10 minutes. Place in greased bowl, cover with a warm cloth, and set in a warm place for 1 hour. Punch down and let it rise again until it doubles its bulk. Form into loaves and place in well-greased pans. Cover and let the dough rise once more until it doubles its bulk again. Bake in preheated 450° F (232° C) oven for 45 minutes. Remove from pans and cool.

✂PERSIMMON COOKIES

Persimmons grew wild in the Mid-Atlantic states to the coast of Florida and in the Midwest from Ohio and Nebraska south to Texas. In season from October to February, they make excellent puddings and cookies.

Ingredients
Persimmons
Egg
Baking soda
Sugar
Shortening
Flour
Chopped walnuts
Raisins
Cinnamon
Cloves
Nutmeg

Utensils
Cookie sheet
Mixing bowl
Measuring containers and
    spoons
Wooden spoon
Flour sifter

RECIPE

Standard
1 cup mashed persimmons
    (3 persimmons)

Metric

1 teaspoon baking soda	5 grams
1 well-beaten egg	
1 cup sugar	240 grams
1/2 cup shortening	120 grams
2 cups flour	280 grams
1 cup walnuts, chopped	125 grams
1 cup raisins	200 grams
1/2 teaspoon each, cinnamon, cloves, nutmeg	1 1/4 grams

METHOD

Cream sugar and shortening. Add mashed persimmon, soda, and egg. Sift flour and spices together and add to creamed mixture. Add raisins and chopped walnuts. Drop by spoonful onto greased cookie sheet. Bake 15 minutes at 350° F (177° C).

Yield: 3 dozen.

❧SOURDOUGH PANCAKES

One of the most precious items taken on the pioneer trail was the sourdough "starter" that was faithfully preserved to make bread or pancakes. The pioneers often resorted to the yeast in the air to make their first batch. We are able to make a good starter with packaged yeast.

Starter Ingredients
Yeast
Sugar
Salt
Eggs
Potato water
Flour
Oil

Utensils
Sauce pan
Bowl, earthenware
Wooden spoon. Do not use
    metal.

STARTER RECIPE

Standard	Metric
2 cups water that a potato has been cooked in	480 ml
1 package yeast	7 grams
1 teaspoon salt	5 grams
1 teaspoon sugar	5 grams
2 eggs beaten	
2 cups all-purpose flour	260 grams
3 tablespoons oil	45 ml

METHOD

Soften yeast in the warm potato water in an *earthenware* bowl. Mix all ingredients and place the bowl away, lightly covered, to ferment. It will take 48 hours. Place starter in jar and refrigerate for use.

PANCAKE RECIPE

Standard	Metric
Mix the night before:	
2 cups starter	480 ml
2 cups warm water	480 ml
2 1/2 cups flour	320 grams
1 tablespoon sugar	15 grams

Cover and let stand in warm place overnight.
In the morning, take 2 cups of the mix and add to the following:

1/3 cup milk	80 ml
1/2 teaspoon salt	3 grams
1 teaspoon soda	5 grams
2 teaspoons sugar	18 grams
(If making waffles, 2 tablespoons oil)	30 ml

Mix well, let stand a few minutes. Make pancakes on a hot greased griddle.

230

🌿PIE CRUST

The secret of a good pie is a good crust. Some people, especially young men, I have noticed, have no trouble rolling out a perfect pie crust with any recipe. One young man I met gave me a few tips that he had learned as a cook in the army.

Ingredients
Flour
Salt
Shortening
Milk

Utensils
9-inch round pie tin
Pastry blender
Rolling pin
Measuring containers and
    spoons
Bowl for mixing
Fork

RECIPE

Standard	*Metric*
2 cups flour	280 grams
1/2 teaspoon salt	3 grams
1/2 cup shortening	120 grams
1/3 cup milk	80 ml

METHOD
Combine flour and salt. Cut shortening into the flour with a pastry blender or 2 knives. Add milk. Mix lightly with a fork. Divide in half. Roll each section into a ball and flatten each slightly. Fold the four sides of each flattened ball toward the center. Turn dough over and *let it rest* while you deal with the other section of dough in the same manner.

Lightly dust counter with flour. Start rolling the dough lightly and evenly from the center. Turn when the round is 6–8 inches in diameter and roll on the other side until it is large and thin enough to fit the pie tin.

Flute the edges before filling with one-crust pie.

Refrigerate remaining dough or use as crust for the top of a 2-crust fruit pie.

❧MOLASSES PUMPKIN PIE

One of the most famous American dishes is pie, especially if it is made from pumpkin. Thanksgiving dinner is not complete without at least one pumpkin pie for dessert. The early colonists ate pumpkin in some form every day. In addition to pie, they used it for bread, puddings, or pancakes. Sometimes they simply boiled it and ate it plain because food was scarce. They sliced it and dried it on racks in the sun to preserve it.

Ingredients	*Utensils*
Milk	Measuring containers
Molasses	Measuring spoons
Pumpkin	Rotary egg beater
Brown sugar	Bowl for mixing
Eggs	
Salt	
Cinnamon	
Ginger	
Cloves	
Unbaked 9″ pie crust	
Nutmeg	

RECIPE

Standard	*Metric*
2 cups milk	480 ml
2 cups pumpkin, or 1 (16 oz) can	450 grams
1/2 cup molasses	120 ml
1/2 cup brown sugar	120 grams
3 eggs, slightly beaten	
1/2 teaspoon salt	3 grams
1/2 teaspoon cloves	3 grams
1 1/2 teaspoons each, nutmeg, cinnamon, ginger	7 grams

METHOD
Preheat oven to 400° F (205° C).

Combine pumpkin, salt, and spices in large bowl. Add slightly beaten eggs, milk, molasses, and sugar. Stir.

Pour into pie shell and bake 50–55 minutes until knife inserted in center comes out clean.

Cool and serve.

TAMALE PIE

The Indians ground masa from parched corn. Masa is specially treated with limewater. Originally they made a paste of masa, salt, and broth and spread it over dried corn husks which were then tied and steamed over boiling water. Instant masa may be purchased at most markets.

Ingredients	*Utensils*
Beef	Skillet
Onion	Bowl
Canned tomatoes	Baking dish, 1 1/2 quart
Canned corn	
Masa harina	
Chili powder	
Olives	
Tomato, fresh	
Cheese	

RECIPE

Standard	*Metric*
2 tablespoons oil	30 ml
1 onion, chopped	125 grams
1/2 lb ground beef	250 grams
1 cup canned tomatoes	240 ml
1 cup canned cream-style corn	240 ml
1 teaspoon salt	5 grams
1 teaspoon chili powder	5 grams
2/3 cup masa harina	50 grams
1/3 cup water or milk	80 ml
1/4 cup ripe olives	
1 fresh tomato	
1/4 cup grated cheese	60 grams

METHOD

Sauté onion in oil in skillet. Add meat. Stir in the vegetables and seasoning. In a bowl mix the masa and water (or milk). Place a thin layer of the masa mixture on the bottom of the baking dish. Pour the meat and vegetables over it. Top with remaining masa mixture. Place olives, sliced tomato, and grated cheese on top of the layer of masa.
Bake for 25 minutes in a 350° F (177° C) oven.
Yield: 4 servings.

✄RYE AND INDIAN BREAD

Often baked in the hearth of colonial kitchens in a cast-iron Dutch oven with coals piled on the lid. It was made from equal parts of cornmeal (Indian meal) and rye flour.

Ingredients	Utensils
All-purpose flour	Mixing bowl
Cornmeal	Sauce pan
Rye flour	Measuring container and
Milk	spoon
Molasses or sorghum	Baking dish, 1 1/2 quart
Yeast	size
Salt	Wooden spoon or electric
	mixer

RECIPE

Standard	Metric
1 package dry yeast	7 grams
1 cup milk	240 ml
1/4 cup molasses	60 ml
3/4 cup rye flour	104 grams
3/4 cup cornmeal	150 grams
1 3/4 cups all-purpose flour	220 grams
or 1 cup all-purpose flour and	140 grams
3/4 cup whole wheat flour	80 grams
3/4 teaspoon salt	4 grams

234

METHOD

In a sauce pan, heat milk, molasses, and salt until warm. In a mixing bowl, mix 1 cup all-purpose flour, 1/2 cup cornmeal, 1/2 cup rye flour, and yeast. Add lukewarm liquids to flour mixture. Beat well with electric mixer at low speed for 3 minutes, or with wooden spoon. Let stand in warm place until doubled in size. Add remaining flour: 3/4 cup whole wheat, 1/4 cup rye, and 1/4 cup cornmeal. Knead on floured board. Cover and let rise in warm place for 1 hour. Place in baking dish and let rise once more. Bake 50 minutes in 325° F (163° C) oven.

❦16❦
New Grains and Old Mills

The seeds of grain sown so many centuries ago in Jarmo have multiplied to well over 334 million metric tons a year. The corn that was first cultivated by Indians in Central America has likewise increased to staggering amounts, and even more rice is cultivated in Asia. Yet agricultural experts are working day and night in laboratories and experimental fields to double the present yield.

The first agricultural revolution that began with the sowing of a few seeds to feed a small village was the most significant event in human history. With it civilization began. The latest agricultural revolution, the "green revolution," has only just begun within the present century. Its results are still uncertain, but its aim is monumental—to feed the population of the whole world with the grains of "miracle seeds" that are disease and drought resistant, contain a higher amount of protein, and have a very high yield.

To date, research institutions that are supported by the Ford and Rockefeller foundations and an international group of world donors have altered sorghum, corn, wheat, and rice by seed selection and repeated crossings of related plants to obtain the desired characteristics. In addition, rye and wheat have been crossed to form a new grain called *triticale*. It contains more protein than wheat or rye, and combines the dis-

At the Institute of Agricultural Research in Ethiopia, agronomist and plant breeder examine triticale plants. *United Nations/Photo by D. Mason.*

ease resistance and productivity of wheat with the hardiness of rye. Bakery products made from its flour have a pleasant, slightly sweet taste.

The green revolution has met resistance. Peasants in many parts of the world are loath to change their age-old methods of farming, and they complain about the cost of the necessary fertilizer, the taste of the rice, or the color of the wheat. The botanists who created the green revolution regret that only 35 percent of the wheat area and 20 percent of the rice area of Asia were planted with the new seeds in 1973, although with them production has greatly increased in India, Pakistan, and the Philippines. Egypt is beginning to plant the new hybrid wheat and additional centers of research in Nigeria, Colombia, and Peru are continuing the work along with those established in Mexico and the United States.

Another movement that has a wider acceptance, especially among young people, is the new concern about the wisest use of whole grains in milling and cooking to retain all of their nutrients and flavor. Grains are a very important part of man's diet. If necessity demanded it, a person could obtain all of the food elements he needs from a diet of grains and milk. How foolish, then, it is to grind all of the vitamins and minerals out of whole grains.

Until the middle of the nineteenth century, whole grains were slowly ground between two stones. At first, as you may recall, the top stone was pushed by hand. Then, in the second century B.C. the Romans used animal power to rotate huge circular stones. Finally, the weight of water dropping on a wheel was the prime mover in mills that were built on streams throughout Europe. Millstones from quarries in France became part of the cargo of ships sailing to the American colonies. The road to the mill was a well-traveled one in every American community. The mill was a meeting place from which spicy news and good-flavored flour were carried home.

Then came the industrial age when speed and mass produc-

Winnowing and sifting grain. U.S. Patent Office. *The Growth of Industrial Art.* Benjamin Butterworth, Ed. Washington: Government Printing Office, 1892.
New York Public Library, Picture Collection.

tion were of the greatest importance. Metal steam-driven rollers were invented, which could produce flour one thousand times faster than the slower-moving grinding stones. But the germ of the grain became heated and oily, clogging up the metal grinding surfaces. It had to be removed—and with it ninety percent of the nutrients of the grain. The new flour was white and starchy. It kept longer without becoming rancid, and it could be baked into a white, light, spongy loaf, minus many vitamins.

The next step—to enrich the flour with some of the vitamins lost in the milling—has only partially satisfied many home cooks and bakers who demand natural stone-ground, full-flavored grain. Consequently, more and more packages advertising stone-ground flour or breads and cereals made of whole grains are appearing on the shelves of many supermarkets to compete with the quantities of natural grains sold in health food stores.

The old water mills are grinding once again. They have been restored to be more than historical landmarks. New companies with new stone mills are going into business all over the country, and some housewives are even grinding their own grain with small electric stone mills. GRAINS ARE IN. They are healthy, nourishing, inexpensive, and fun to use in cooking.

A HOMEMADE GRANOLA

A nourishing breakfast is sometimes a problem for those who have to rush off to school or work early in the morning. Granola may be the answer for those who want the nourishment of a whole grain cereal, yet do not have the time to cook one each morning. Granola bars may be made on the weekend and stored in plastic bags or wax paper ready for each morning or even an afternoon snack.

Ingredients

Rolled oats
Barley flakes
Rye flakes
Wheat germ
Sesame seeds
Raisins
Any dried fruit, apples, apricots
Shredded coconut
Bran
Salad oil
Honey
Molasses or brown sugar
Powdered milk

Utensils

Measuring containers and
  spoons
Large bowl
Wooden spoon
Large baking pan or
  cookie sheet

RECIPE

Standard	Metric
1 cup coconut	113 grams
2 cups rolled oats	200 grams
2 cups barley flakes	200 grams
1 cup rye flakes	100 grams
1 cup wheat germ	75 grams
1/2 cup sesame seeds	80 grams
1/2 cup bran	50 grams
1 cup chopped dried fruit	250 grams
1 1/2 cups raisins	250 grams
1/2 cup powdered milk	125 grams
1 cup honey	240 ml
1 cup molasses	240 ml
1/2 cup salad oil	120 ml

METHOD

Mix all of the dry ingredients in a large bowl. Blend and heat the honey, molasses, and salad oil. Add to the mixture in the bowl until the liquids coat the flakes. Spread out on cookie sheet. Bake 45 minutes to 1 hour in 275° F (135° C) oven.

Cool, cut into squares, and store in plastic bags or wax paper.

❧TRITICALE RAISIN MUFFINS

Ingredients
Triticale flour
All-purpose wheat flour
Baking powder
Salad oil
Milk
Sugar
Raisins
Egg

Utensils
Muffin tins
Large bowl
Medium bowl
Flour sifter
Measuring containers and
    spoons
Wooden spoon

RECIPE

Standard	*Metric*
1 cup triticale flour	130 grams
1 cup all-purpose flour, sifted	128 grams
3 teaspoons baking powder	15 grams
1/2 teaspoon salt	3 grams
1/4 cup salad oil	60 ml
1 cup milk	220 ml
1 cup raisins	160 grams
1 egg	
1 tablespoon sugar	15 grams

METHOD

Sift the triticale and all-purpose flour together into a large bowl. Add sugar, salt, baking powder, and blend well. Lightly beat egg with a fork in medium-size bowl. Add oil, milk, and stir. Add to dry ingredients. Add raisins. Stir just enough to moisten flour. Mixture should be lumpy. Pour into greased muffin tins. Bake in 400° F (205° C) oven for 20 minutes.

Yield: 18.

❧MILLET AND GROUND ROUND CASSEROLE

Ingredients	Utensils
Ground beef	Sauce pan
Onion	Skillet
Garlic salt	Knife for chopping
Cayenne pepper	Measuring containers and
Tomato soup	spoons
Millet	1 1/2 quart casserole
Salt	
Cheese	

RECIPE

Standard	Metric
1 cup whole millet	200 grams
2 cups water	480 ml
1/2 lb ground round	250 grams
1 medium onion, chopped	125-150 grams
2 teaspoons garlic salt	10 grams
1 teaspoon cayenne pepper	5 grams
1 can (10 3/4 oz) tomato soup	305 grams
2 tablespoons oil	30 ml
1/2 cup shredded cheese	100 grams

METHOD

Pour the whole grain millet into boiling water in sauce pan. Reduce heat to medium and cook until the liquid is absorbed and the grains are fluffy, about 30 minutes.

Sauté onion in skillet in 2 tablespoons oil. Add meat and cook until brown. Season with garlic salt and cayenne pepper.

Place a layer of cooked millet on the bottom of casserole or baking dish. Add meat, onion, and soup. Place another layer of millet over meat mixture. Top with cheese and bake in 350° F (177° C) oven for 20 minutes.

Serves 4.

🌿WHOLE WHEAT ROLLS

Ingredients	Utensils
Yeast	Mixing bowl
Sugar	Measuring cup or metric
Honey	measuring container
Butter	Measuring spoons
Salt	Wooden spoon
Egg	Sauce pan
Whole wheat flour	Rotary egg beater
Raisins	2 Muffin tins
Water	

RECIPE

Standard	Metric
1 oz yeast	7 grams
1 tablespoon sugar	15 grams
1/4 cup lukewarm water	60 ml
4 tablespoons butter	60 grams
1/4 cup honey	60 ml
2 teaspoons salt	10 grams
1 beaten egg	
3 1/2 cups whole wheat flour	600 grams
2/3 cup raisins	132 grams

METHOD

Dissolve the yeast in 1/4 cup (60 ml) of lukewarm water. Add 1 tablespoon of sugar to the yeast mixture.

Boil 1 cup (240 ml) water in sauce pan. Add butter, 1/4 cup honey, and salt. Let it stand until it is lukewarm.

Beat the egg with rotary egg beater. When the boiled water is lukewarm, add the beaten egg and yeast mixture.

Place the flour and raisins in a large bowl. Combine all the mixtures and beat well. If the dough is too stiff, add a small amount of lukewarm water.

Place the bowl of dough in a warm place. It is not necessary to knead it. When it has doubled in size, beat with wooden

244

spoon. Place a small piece of dough (the size of a golf ball) in each well of a muffin tin. Let rise again until each piece of dough has doubled in size.

Bake in a 375° F (191° C) oven for 15 minutes.

Yield: 25 rolls.

❧SKILLET QUICK BREAD

Ingredients	*Utensils*
Barley flour	Mixing bowl
Whole wheat flour	Measuring cups or metric
White cornmeal	measuring containers
Brown sugar	Measuring spoons
Eggs	Wooden spoon
Milk	Skillet
Baking powder	
Salt	
Bran	

RECIPE

Standard	*Metric*
1/3 cup barley flour	60 grams
1/3 cup whole wheat flour	50 grams
1/3 cup white cornmeal	65 grams
1/3 cup bran	20 grams
1/3 cup brown sugar	80 grams
2 eggs	
2 cups milk	480 ml.
4 teaspoons baking powder	20 grams
1 teaspoon salt	5 grams

METHOD

Combine the flours, bran, sugar, baking powder, and salt in large mixing bowl. Add the well-beaten eggs. Add the milk and stir with wooden spoon. Pour into a greased skillet. Bake in preheated oven 350° F (177° C) for 30 minutes. Serve with jam and butter.

Appendix

The following table indicates the quantities of the principal grains grown in the world, the quantities grown in the United States, and the percentage of the United States production to world production.

Agricultural products (grain) in million metric tons

Production

	U.S.	WORLD	% U.S.
Wheat	42	334.5	12.6
Oats	10	51.3	19.5
Corn	141.6	286.7	49.4
Barley	9.2	138.7	6.6
Rice	4.2	308.8	1.4

Source: *World Almanac 1975*

States leading in the production of grain in the United States in order of production in 1971

Iowa	1,180,140,000 bushels
Illinois	1,037,340,000
Indiana	534,373,000
Minnesota	475,175,000
Nebraska	455,260,000
Kansas	437,150,000
Ohio	318,814,000

Missouri	272,096,000
Wisconsin	203,603,000
South Dakota	123,234,000
Michigan	115,600,000
Kentucky	94,402,000

Total crop in all states 5,540,253,000 bushels.

States leading in wheat production in 1971

Kansas	312,605,000 bushels
North Dakota	285,231,000
Washington	118,921,000
Montana	112,011,000
Nebraska	107,436,000
Colorado	70,920,000
Oklahoma	69,500,000
South Dakota	68,768,000
Idaho	50,623,000
Illinois	43,525,000
Ohio	42,674,000

Total U. S. Crop: 1,639,516,000 bushels.

States leading in production of rice in 1971

Texas	22,932,000 cwt.
Arkansas	21,830,000
Louisiana	19,836,000
California	17,212,000

Total United States Crop: 84,315,000 cwt.

Oats

Minnesota	177,000,000 bushels
South Dakota	125,766,000
North Dakota	110,825,000
Wisconsin	93,635,000
Iowa	91,450,000

Total United States Crop: 538,474,000 bushels.

Rye

South Dakota	12,672,000 bushels
North Dakota	9,750,000
Nebraska	6,580,000
Minnesota	4,590,000
Kansas	2,640,000

Total United States Crop: 59,935,000 bushels

Barley

North Dakota	99,810,000 bushels
Montana	58,800,000
California	57,611,000
Minnesota	40,740,000
Idaho	38,830,000

Total United States Crop: 462,484,000 bushels

Sorghum grain

Texas	303,004,000 bushels
Kansas	182,896,000
Nebraska	125,160,000
Missouri	47,700,000

Total United States Crop: 895,349,000

Metric Conversion Chart for Grains

Barley (1 cup)
Whole	200 grams
Flour	175 grams
Flakes	100 grams

Oats (1 cup)
Steel cut	200 grams
Flakes	100 grams

Millet (1 cup)
Whole	200 grams
Flour	175 grams

Rye (1 cup)
Flakes	100 grams
Flour	150 grams
Whole	175 grams

Cornmeal (1 cup) 200 grams

Wheat (1 cup)
Bran	50 grams
Germ	75 grams
Flour (unsifted all-purpose)	140 grams
(sifted all-purpose)	128 grams
(sifted cake and pastry)	120 grams
Bulgur	150 grams

Rice (1 cup)
	240 grams
Flour	130 grams

Triticale (1 cup)
Flour	130 grams

Conversion Chart
STANDARD TO METRIC

Liquid

1 teaspoon	5 ml
1 tablespoon	15 ml
1 oz (fluid)	30 ml
1/4 cup	60 ml
1/3 cup	80 ml
1/2 cup	120 ml
2/3 cup	160 ml
3/4 cup	180 ml
1 cup	240 ml

Sugar Granulated

1/4 cup	60 grams
1/2 cup	120 grams
1 cup	240 grams

Butter

1 tablespoon	15 grams
1/4 cup	60 grams
1/2 cup	120 grams
1 cup	240 grams

Salt, Baking Powder, Cornstarch

1 teaspoon	5 grams
1 tablespoon	15 grams

Ground Spices, Pepper

1 teaspoon	2 1/2 grams
1 tablespoon	7 1/2 grams

Vegetables
1 lb fresh	500 grams
1 oz frozen or canned	28.3 grams

Meat and Fish
1 lb	500 grams
1 cup (8 oz) diced	250 grams

Cheese
1 lb	500 grams
1 cup, grated (4 oz)	125 grams

Cooking Temperatures

$0°$ Centigrade = $32°$ Fahrenheit

$100°$ Centigrade = $212°$ Fahrenheit

(Fahrenheit temperature -32) $\times$ $5/9$ = Centigrade temperature

$275°$ F = $135°$ C	$400°$ F = $205°$ C
$300°$ F = $149°$ C	$425°$ F = $218°$ C
$325°$ F = $163°$ C	$450°$ F = $232°$ C
$350°$ F = $177°$ C	$475°$ F = $246°$ C
$375°$ F = $191°$ C	$500°$ F = $260°$ C

Recipe Language

For Cooking:

Bake: To cook by dry heat in an oven.

Blanch: To plunge food into a pan of boiling water and follow by a quick cooling in cold water, usually to remove skins from fruits or vegetables, or to parboil.

Boil: To cook in liquid that has reached the boiling temperature.

Broil: To cook under a flame or heating unit. If this is done under the top heating element in an oven, the door should be partially open to allow air to circulate.

Deep Fry: To cook food by immersion in melted fat which has reached a high temperature.

Fry: To cook food in fat or oil.

Poach: To simmer food in liquid that is below the boiling point.

Roast: To cook meat or poultry in dry heat in an oven.

Sauté: To cook food in a skillet with just enough oil or fat to prevent the food from sticking. The food should be dry and the oil hot.

Scald: To heat a liquid, such as milk, up to the simmering point. No bubbling of the liquid should occur even on the bottom of the pan.

Simmer: To cook food in hot liquid that has not reached the boiling point. Only small bubbles should appear on the bottom of the pan.

Steam: To cook food above steam. No water contacts the food. A double boiler or steamer may be used or a colander placed over a pan of boiling water.

Stew: To cook food long and slowly in a simmering liquid.

For Mixing:

Beat: To make a smooth mixture by vigorously stirring it around and around with a spoon, beater, or electric mixer.

Blend: To thoroughly combine two or more ingredients.

Cream: To blend sugar and fat (margarine, butter, lard, or vegetable shortening) together until it is smooth and creamy with a spoon, rubber spatula, or electric mixer.

Cut in: To cut fat into flour with two knives or a pastry blender.

Fold in: To combine a fluffy, beaten mixture (egg whites, whipped cream, whipped gelatin) with a solid mixture, as a cake batter. Gently move a spoon or rubber spatula through the center of the two mixtures, down to the bottom of the bowl and up on the sides. Repeat until the entire mixture is blended, but no air is lost in the fluffier mixture.

Season: To add salt, pepper, and/or spices to improve the flavor of food.

Whip: To beat rapidly in order to add air to cream, eggs, or gelatin.

For Cooking With Flour:

Batter: A mixture of flour, liquid, and eggs that may be poured or dropped from a spoon.

Cereal: The name for the grains that are used as food by mankind, such as wheat, corn, barley, millet, oats, rice, rye, and sorghum.

Dough: A mixture of flour and liquid, and sometimes shortening, that is thick enough to roll or push into shape.

Flour: A powder that results from the grinding of cereal grains.

Gluten: A protein that is in wheat flour. It has a setting and stretching power that is used in making bread and cakes.

Leavening agent: That which makes bread dough or cake batter light and spongy. Baking powder, yeast, and baking soda are leavening agents.

Baking powder: A mixture of chemicals that will give off carbon dioxide when it is mixed with a liquid and heated, causing bread or cake to rise. Baking powder is made of soda, a dry powder, and cornstarch. It is used in making quick breads or cakes. *Baking soda* is used with recipes that include buttermilk or sour milk, as they contain the required acid.

Yeast: A kind of plant that seeks nourishment in starch and sugar and multiplies rapidly in warmth and moisture. When yeast is mixed into bread dough, the gluten in the wheat flour stretches because carbon dioxide gas bubbles are formed by the action of the yeast. The gas disappears when the product is baked but the risen shape remains.

Knead: The purpose of kneading is to thoroughly blend the ingredients and to develop the gluten to form an elastic network that is spread throughout the dough. To knead by hand, form the dough toward you, then press it away with the heel of your hand. Turn the dough one-fourth of the way around toward you. Fold it over, push it away, repeat the process until the dough is smooth, elastic, and shiny.

Masa flour: Flour that has been ground from cooked corn kernels. It must be used quickly because it sours quickly. A commercially prepared flour called Instant Masa may be kept longer.

Pastry: A mixture of flour, liquid, and fat which forms a crust or base for pies, tarts, or flans.

Pasta: A mixture of flour, liquid, fat or oil, and sometimes eggs, to make spaghetti, macaroni, or other Italian noodles.

Roux: A blend of flour and butter that has been cooked for a minute or two on low heat. It is used as a base for sauces.

Rest the dough: To set it aside without handling it so the gluten within the dough will relax, making the dough less elastic and easier to handle.

Rise: Allow the dough to double in size because of the action of yeast in warmth, or of baking powder when the product is baked.

Bibliography

Bailey, Anthony. *The Light in Holland.* Alfred A. Knopf, N.Y., 1970

Bothwell, Jean. *The Story of India.* Harcourt Brace & Co., N.Y., 1952

Bozart, L. & Kenimerer, David. *Economic History of the American People.* Longmans Green, N.Y., 1947

Child, Julia. *French Chef Cookbook.* Alfred A. Knopf, N.Y., 1968

Davis, Wm. Stearns. *Life on a Medieval Barony.* Harper & Row, N.Y., 1928

Doblar, La Vinia. *Customs and Holidays Around the World.* Fleet Press Corp., N.Y., 1962

Grossinger, Jennie. *Art of Jewish Cooking.* Random House, N.Y., 1958

Faulkner, Harold. *American Economic History.* Harper & Row, N.Y., 1960

Giles, Dorothy. *Singing Valleys, The Story of Corn.* Random House, N.Y., 1940

Halverhout, Heleen. *Dutch Cooking.* Amsterdam, De Driehoek

Hawkes, Jacquetta. *World of the Past, Vol. 1.* Alfred A. Knopf, N.Y., 1975

Kellner, Leon. *Austria of the Austrians, Hungary of the Hungarians.* Sir Isaac Pittman & Son, 1914

Kramer, Samuel N. *History Begins at Sumer.* Doubleday, N.Y., 1959

Kraus, Barbara, (Ed.). *United Nations Cookbook.* Simon & Schuster, N.Y., 1970

Lee, Jim, *Jim Lee's Chinese Cookbook.* Harper & Row, N.Y., 1968

McClure, C.H. & Yarborough, W.H. *United States of America.* Laidlaw Bros., N.Y., 1945

MacKay, Alistair I. *Farming and Gardening in the Bible.* Rodale Press, Emmaus, Pa., 1952

Memde, Helen. *The African Heritage Cookbook.* Macmillan, N.Y., 1971

Mills, Dorothy. *The Middle Ages.* G.P. Putnam & Sons, N.Y., 1935

Montagne, Prosper. *Larousse Gastronomique.* Crown Publishing Co., N.Y., 1973

Murray, Margaret A. *The Splendor That Was Egypt*. Praeger Publ., N.Y., 1973

Norman, Barbara. *The Spanish Cookbook*. Atheneum, N.Y., 1966

Orton, Mildred E. *Cooking with Whole Grains*. Farrar, Straus, Giroux, Inc., N.Y., 1951

Root, Waverley: *The Food of France*. Alfred A. Knopf, N.Y., 1958

Sandler, Bea. *The African Cookbook*. Thom. Y. Crowell, N.Y., 1972

Sarvis, Shirley. *A Taste of Portugal*. Ch. Scribner & Sons, N.Y., 1967

Spier, Peter. *Of Dikes and Windmills*. Doubleday & Co., N.Y., 1969

Stavrianos, Leften. *The World Since 1950*. Prentice-Hall, Inc., Englewood Cliffs, New Jersey, 1975

Tannahill, Leah. *Food in History*. Stein & Day, N.Y., 1973

Time-Life Books. *Foods of the World*. Time, Inc., N.Y., 1968

Woman's Day Encyclopedia of Cooking. Fawcett Publishing, Co., N.Y., 1973

MAGAZINES

National Geographic Magazine
 Lafay, "Vikings," April 1970
 Warwick, "Farmers Since the Days of Noah," April 1927
This England, Winter 1972
 Cottam, Hazel, "Pancake Tuesday"
 Rees, Catherine, "Shrovetide Football"

Index